Raymond James

The Secrets of Life

Raymond James

The Secrets of Life

Blessed Hope Publishing

Imprint

Cover image: www.ingimage.com

Publisher:
Blessed Hope Publishing
is a trademark of
International Book Market Service Ltd., member of OmniScriptum Publishing Group
17 Meldrum Street, Beau Bassin 71504, Mauritius
Printed at: see last page
ISBN: 978-613-7-97413-1

THE

SECRET

OF

LIFE

RAYMOND E. JAMES

CONTENT

INTRODUCTION

Life itself and everything in it depend on the law which govern them which is a secret to many people because they did not have access to the knowledge behind life.

The secret of life is hidden everywhere in the form of the law that govern nature and it is only the people that earnestly seek for it that will find it if they are not too blind to see it.

Life is beautiful when things are going the way we want it, but life can be bad if things are going against us. There are rules that govern everything in life and if we live by these rules, life will be good for us but if we live against it, we will individually have a sad story to tell.

Life is a secret only to those that don't seek for knowledge for if you seek for knowledge and you understand and apply the knowledge, many things that appear as a secret will not be a secret to you. You will live a better life and become a better person by living in accord with the law that governs life.

There are many stories about how life begin and about life itself. Some are reasonable while some are bizarre. Everyone are entitle to their opinion if the opinion is not hostile to life but a wrong opinion cannot become right, even if everybody believe it to be right and a right opinion cannot become wrong, even if everybody did not believe it.

Your opinion about the beginning of life may not agree with the opinion of this book. If your opinion is not in agreement with this book, read the book for knowledge and if you don't want to read it for knowledge, read it for fun and amuse yourself with the story about life.

Some people view life from the angle of religion and see one to be a Christian, the other to be a Muslim and one to be Buddhist, the other to be a Hindu. Some people view life from the angle of education and see one to be literate and the other to be illiterate. Some people view life from the angle of money and see one to be rich and the other to be poor. Some people view life from the angle of God and see one to be a saint and the other to be a sinner.

A true human see all life to be one be it a Christian, a Muslim, a Buddhist or a Hindu. A true human see all life to be one whether a person is literate or illiterate. A true human see all life to be one whether one person is rich or the other is poor. A true human see all life to be one whether a person is a saint or a sinner for everything and everyone are a part of life whether we like it or not.

Let us all have respect for life and tolerate everyone and everything that is part of life and learn to live by the rule that bring life and shun the thought, the word and the act that bring death or lead to death.

Life is a school that teach great knowledge about itself. To some people, the experience of the school of life is good and to others, the experience of the school of life is bad. Life is bad to many people because they did not understand what the school of life is teaching them which appear as a secret to them.

If any person understand the law that govern life and live by it, life will be easy for the person but if any person is ignorant of the law that govern life or neglect to live by the law that govern life, life will be bad for the person.

To experience life by itself so as to learn from it take years of learning but it is easy to learn and it take a short time to learn the experience of life that another person have taken years to learn. If you choose to learn the experience of life all by yourself without looking to the experience of another person, that is a choice you make for yourself and you may live to tell the story that it is better to learn from the experience of another person than to learn for yourself the rigor of an experience all by yourself.

People that are rich live by the law that govern riches, people that are in good health live by the law that govern good health and people that are living a meaningful life live by the law that govern life. Whatever you desire in life, if you live by the law that govern it, you will attain it.

PART 1

THE ABSOLUTE KNOWLEDGE

THE

BEGINNING

OF

LIFE

1

In the beginning was the word and the word was with God and the word was God – Saint John

THE ARGUMENT

The beginning of life seem to defy answer which cause argument between different set of people. The major argument is between the theist, those that believe in God and the atheist, those that believe that there is no God which lead to different concept about how life begin.

Different people wonder about where life came from which make different theory to spring up about the origin of life through the study of nature and the study of the belief of different people about the origin of life.

Some people think about the starting point of life and about who or what create the creator of life and about who or what create the creator of the creator up to the point of who started the creation of the creator. When anyone think about these questions that seem to defy answer, such one may think that he or she is thinking heresy, that is term as a crime against God by the religionist or that one is going against the will of the creator by trying to find out the origin of life or one may think himself or herself to be stupid for having such question in mind.

If anyone have any question that is not answered concerning any area of life, the question will always pave way for doubt within the person's mind especially when it have to do with the beginning of life and the reality of the starting point of life and about life itself as long as the question remain in the person's mind and is not answered to the level of the person understanding.

If one is not convince about the origin of life and how life started, one will always drift in various teaching about the reality of life and about the starting point of life. Such one will find it difficult to stay with a belief for a long period of time, sometime believing that there is a creator and sometime becoming confused if there is a creator of life when the person come across a n argument that outweigh his or her belief about life.

To believe is to be convince and if one is not convince, it will be difficult for one to believe which make argument to spring between those that believe in a creator and those that did not believe in a creator.

Many religion personify the intelligence that create life because the Bible say that God create man in his own image and likeness and other holy book attribute God to human form.

The starting point of life is omniscient, omnipotent, and omnipresent and words cannot perfectly describe it to the understanding of everyone due to the limitation of words to describe something that is beyond the perceptive capacity of the brain.

Despite the fact that the brain cannot perfectly understand the origin of life and the intelligence that create life because words are too limited to describe something that is beyond the perceptive capacity of the brain, we still have to use our intellect to use words to describe the origin of life and the intelligence that create life to the best of our ability to use words to describe life.

Let us use the universe to illustrate the intelligence behind creation and have a glimpse of life and how it is beyond the perceptive capacity of the brain.

There are millions of galaxies in the universe and one galaxy has billions of stars in it. Our planet earth is one of the nine planets that orbit our star, the sun. If one should say that the universe is very big, how big it is will be beyond the perceptive capacity of the brain but when one describe how big the universe is bit by bit, then one will be able to grasp how big the universe is to an extent.

Your town is big and you can imagine how big your town is. Many towns make up your state and you can imagine how big your state is. Many states make up your country and it will take some thinking for you to imagine how big your country is. Many countries make up your continent and for you to imagine how big your continent is will take a lot of calculative thinking. Few continent make up the world and you can see that the word "few" have belittle a continent to the understanding of many people and it have also belittle the world and if you look at the world from a picture, the world that is so big have been made so small by a picture. Now imagine our planet earth as one of the nine planets that orbit the sun. Can you see how words have make something so big to become small and the sun is bigger than the earth and the earth is like a speck if you compare it to the universe. The sun is a star and it is one of the billions of stars in one galaxy. Imagine the sun that is bigger than the earth to be one of the billions of stars in one galaxy. Can you catch up with the imagination? Millions of galaxies is what make up the universe and I believe this will be beyond the imagination of everyone. To simplify it, it will take four years, if we travel from our planet earth at the speed of light to reach the nearest star to our star the sun. If we assume that it will take four years to travel between two close star in a galaxy, how long do you think that it will take to travel between the farthest star apart in a galaxy? If you say that it will take a very long time, what will you say to the distance between two close galaxy and how will you describe the distance between the millions of galaxies in the universe. You can see that there are no words that can describe the universe to the understanding of everyone and any words that we use to describe the universe will belittle the universe.

If there are no words that can perfectly describe the universe, do you think that there are no words that can describe the intelligence behind the creation of the universe to the understanding of everyone. For comparison, it is the human brain that design and create the computer. We can analyse the computer, take it apart and bring it together again but the human brain that design it is beyond the understanding of human, especially when it have to do with the issue of the mind and how faith which is an aspect of the mind heal some people of a disease that defy any cure.

THE MAJOR VERSION

Science, Philosophy, and Religion are the major branches that hold many views, many concept, many ideology and many believe together in their different perspective are not in agreement with each other about the source of life. Although anywhere you go, you will see disagreement between an organization, a sect, a group of people and down to the family unit.

Science see the source of life as a pure energy, Philosophy see the source of life as the universal mind and Religion see the source of life as God. When I say Science, I mean the group of people that believe only in what the eyes can see and what that can be experimented. When I say Philosophy, I mean the group of people that are atheist. And when I say Religion, I mean the group of people that believe in supernatural power or a supreme deity.

Let us use an illustration to see the argument between Science, Philosophy, and Religion:

A pyramid has three sides and if the three sides of the pyramid have three different color, you will think that the color of the side of the pyramid you are seeing is the color of the other two sides if you did not bother to see the other two sides of the pyramid to see whether they are of the same color.

Let us assume that three people journey from a distance country to see what the pyramid look like so as to go back to their country and tell the people in their country about a pyramid that they hear that is bigger than anything in the world. If the first person journey to the pyramid through the north-west of the pyramid and if the color of this side of the pyramid is bright green and the land in front of it is a grass land. The first person will go back to their country with the believe that the pyramid is bright green in color with a grassland. If the second person journey to the pyramid through the north-east of the pyramid and if the color of this side of the pyramid is gray and the land in front of it is a desert. The second person will go back to their country with the believe that the pyramid is gray in color with the land in front of it to be a desert. If the third person journey to the pyramid through the south-west of the pyramid and if the color of this side of the pyramid is dark green and the land in front of it is a forest. The third person will go back to their country with the believe that the pyramid is dark green in color and the land in front of it to be a forest. If the three people were to write a sentence each concerning the pyramid: The first person may write that the pyramid is the biggest thing in the world that is bright green in color with a grassland. The second person may write that there is nothing as big as the pyramid in the world that is colored gray with a desert land. The third person may write that there is nobody that can describe anything as big as the pyramid that is dark green in color with a forest in the front.

You can see that the three of them describe the pyramid with each of their opinion base on their observation. If a strong argument should come up between the three of them and you have not seen a pyramid before nor have the idea of what a pyramid look like, which of the three will you say is correct? It is wrong for anyone to stand as a judge and judge others over what he or she have not seen nor understand. It is better to remain silent than to judge what he or she did not know base on the reasonable argument of others.

THE BEGINNING ACOORDING TO SCIENCE

Science theorize that life start with a big bang about twenty billions years ago to form the universe and the universe begin to expand since then. The universe expand to form each galaxy and each galaxy form billions of stars. Dense nebula condense to form large mass that form planet that are attracted through centripetal force that make them to revolve round the sun. Earth was form along with other planet that revolve round the sum.

On earth, abiotic synthesis of gaseous matter start to develop. The gaseous matter reacted on each other to synthesize complex gaseous matter that reacted on each other to form various mineral matter. The mineral matter reacted on each other and synthesize organic molecule and the organic molecule reacted on each other to form complex organic molecule. The complex organic molecule develop to form a virus which is the border line between living and non living matter. The virus is the border line because it did not have structure like a cell but exist as a coiled nucleic acid enclose in a protein coat. The virus can only exist inside a cell as a living unit and outside a cell it exist as a crystal that is non living. The virus develop into a prokaryotic cell which is the first living thing. The prokaryotic cell develop into two types of cells, the archaebacteria and the eubacteria. Archaebacteria develop into plant and eubacteria develop into animal but many scientist believe that archaebacteria become extinct and life pass through eubacteria.

Science theorize that it take a long time after earth was form for living things to appear on earth which is a period over billions of years and another long time for life to develop to the human stage, the apex of evolution. Christianity and religion that are in agreement with Christianity did not believe in evolution base on the Bible that say that God completed creation in six days. But the Bible say that a day of God is a thousand years of man – second Peter, chapter 3 verse 8 and the Bhagavad gita also report the same thing. If a day of God is a thousand years of man and the Bible say that God completed creation in six days, it means that the six days that God created everything in the earth is six thousand years of man for God to create everything in the earth. If God created everything in the earth for six thousand years, what was God doing for six thousand years? Is it not directing evolution?

THE BEGINNING ACCORDING TO RELIGION

Religion spring from two category. The Hindu category and the Jewish category mix up with the traditional believe of different races.
Every religion that are from the same category have the same set of believe but their mode of worship can be different from each other and some can be as different as black and white.

People also spring from two race, the mongoloid which are the white race and the negroid which are the black race and from these two race spring different color of people. These two race can be trace to the creation story of the

Bible. The Bible state that Adam and Eve were the first human created and this can be true but at the time when only Adam and Eve and their sons, Cain and Abel were on earth, there was another race of people that Cain ran to after killing his brother Abel out of anger due to jealousy.

Some Christian sect are defending the Bible by saying that the people that Cain run to are the descendant of Adam and Eve. If they were the descendant of Adam and Eve, why did the Bible not mention that they were the descendant of Adam and Eve because the Bible always give the account of people of every period of time. At this period of time, the Bible only mentioned Adam and Eve and their sons Cain and Abel.

Some sect assume that Adam and Eve also have daughters that were not mention, since it is not a custom to give account of daughters. If we assume that they were the extension of Adam and Eve which should be the extension of the daughters of Adam and Eve, who impregnate the daughter since it is not Abel that impregnated them to make them a people.

At the beginning according to Science, the land mass was together and it start drifting apart from a period of time to form each continent and the land mass is still drifting for example, North America and Europe presently drift at about the rate of 2 cm per year. This support the Bible that at the beginning, the race of people were not far from each other which make them to mix and form difference race of people that occupy different continent. At the early days of religion, the continent have not drift far from each other like this our present time.

In the days of King Solomon, people journey from other part of the world as recorded by the Bible without the use of a mechanical vehicle to hear the wisdom of King Solomon which support that the continent was then close together. Despite that Science and the Bible seem to be against each other, they prove the truth in each other because the Bible supported Science in some area and Science supported the Bible in some area. If you look deep into the Bible, you will see that it is a book that is in agreement with Science and Philosophy.

There are three types of religion base on their different belief. The monotheist religion believe in a supreme God, the polytheist religion believe in the existence of many gods as the manifestation of the supreme God and the atheist religion did not believe in God.

Every religion have their own story of how life started which hang on either the Jewish creation story or the Hindus creation story which are the region of human starting point. Some stories are reasonable while some are bizarre.

All holy books including the Bible are written in metaphor, personification and hyperbole. Metaphor is a word use in an imagination way to describe something in order to show that the two have the same quality and make the description more powerful, for example, she have a heart of stone. Personification is the practice of representing object quality, etc. as human being, for example, the serpent deceive Eve to eat the fruit of knowledge. Hyperbole is a way of speaking or writing that make something sound better, more interesting, or more dangerous etc. than it really is. The phrase "God is a jealous God" is use to deter people from the worship of idol and make people devote to the worship of God for the intelligence that create everything cannot be jealous of anything. The phrase "God is angry" is a personification that gave the intelligence that create life human characteristic so that everyone can have the fear of it and keep the law of life. Anger is a negative human emotion that cause destruction and a perfect being can never be angry and the intelligence behind life is beyond perfection. A temple that is called the house of God is a place that people come together in the name of the worship of God and to study the law that govern life as they understand it. The intelligence behind life is omnipresent, meaning that God is everywhere and if God is everywhere mean that God did not dwell in a house. The revelation that was reveal to John in the Bible is a mystical figure of speech just like the dream that was given to King Pharaoh was in figure of speech that was beyond the understanding of king Pharaoh and every wise men of that time except Joseph. It is written in revelation that God send his angel and present it in signs – Revelation chapter 1 verse 1. This show the Revelation has it own interpretation.

Good and evil are human characteristic and nature which represent life will give to anyone what anyone give to it which make the Bible say that God is good to some people and evil to some people for God is in the heart of everyone.

The creation story of the Bible is synonymous with the evolution theory of science with the missing link as evolution, although the evolution theory of science have a lot of detail base on the experimental nature of scientist for the scientist don't believe anything without probing and investigating it unlike the religionist that accept everything without questioning it.

The evolution theory of science, that is the order of evolution are of the same order with the creation story of the Bible which mean that if we ignore the word "evolution", Science and the Bible are saying the same thing using different language to say it.

The creation story of the Bible and the evolution theory of Science came up at different era and they are similar in order for they both start from the non living to living things, yet the disciple of Science and the disciple of the Bible are not in agreement with each other base on the fact that the scientist did not believe in God because they cannot experiment God. But if the theory of evolution is in agreement either in part or whole with the creation story of the Bible with the missing link that one thing evolve to another, is evolution not proving the reality of the Bible? Will anyone say that the Bible copy evolution? The Bible have existed for a long time before the theory of evolution came up and it will be bizarre for anyone to say that evolution copy the Bible.

Those that are against evolution say that if evolution is true, human suppose to have evolve to another being, that evolution suppose not to stop but it is possible for evolution to programme itself to stop at the stage of human, the apex of evolution. If anyone consider the stage of human intellectual development, the human brain is evolving if we consider how the brain is making the world a global village.

The monotheist believes that there is only one God and the polytheist believes that other gods are the manifestation of the supreme God. In John chapter 1 verse 1 to verse 3, it says that in the beginning was the word and the word was with God and the word was God. Is this not similar to the polytheist that say every other gods are the manifestation of the supreme God? If life start from a source, will one not say that it is this source that all life came from and all gods also came from this source as the manifestation of life. There is nothing in life that is not created to serve a particular purpose. The good gods serve to bless the good and the evil gods serve to punish the evil. Although it can be extremely difficult to believe in these gods but if we are living a good life, we will not have business with the evil gods and the evil gods will not have business with us.

Moses, the author of the creation story in the Bible is considered to be myth by some people despite the archaeological evidence that support that Moses existed at a particular period of time and the theory of evolution that is similar to the creation story of Moses is a prove that Moses existed at a particular period of time.

Moses begin the creation story by saying that in the beginning God created the heaven and the earth. By using the word "heaven", he may refer to the galaxies and when we include the earth, he may refer to our solar system. The heaven and the earth that Moses said was the beginning was not included in the six days of creation. No period of time was assign to the beginning by Moses which mean that the beginning which are millions of galaxies was beyond Moses imagination. The six days of creation reveal by Moses started from when the earth was without form and void and darkness was all over it.

In the beginning, God created the heaven and the earth. This beginning of creation is beyond time and space which mean that it is beyond the perception capacity of the brain because Moses could not give time to it and science could not measure it space.

The first day of creation according to Moses, God create light and bring a division between the light and the darkness that was in existence and God call the light day and the darkness God call night. According to Science light first came into existence by the big bang which mean that Science and the Bible agree that it is light that first came into life.

The second day of creation, God created the heaven that separate the water filled earth into two portion. The upper portion God call heaven and this heaven is different from the stellar heaven which Moses say was the beginning.

The water filled earth was not a liquid water, it is a gaseous water similar to mist.

The third day of creation, God created land from the water that was below the heaven and bring the water into one place by condensing the gaseous water and call it sea. And God commanded vegetation to shoot forth from the land according to their kind and fruit yielding tree according to their kind.

The fourth day of creation, God created the sun and the moon. This may seem not to agree with Science for Science theorize that the sun came to life before the earth. Moses is not wrong by saying that God created the sun on the fourth day because the sun appear on the fourth day when the gaseous water in heaven condense to form cloud on the fourth day which make the sun to be visible on the fourth day. This mean that God condense the gaseous water in the fourth day which appear to Moses as the creation of the sun and the moon on the fourth day.

The fifth day of creation, God created all form of flying creature to fly over the face of the earth. God proceed to create the great sea monster according to their kind.

The sixth day of creation which is the last day of creation, God created the domestic animal and all moving animals and the wild beast according to their kind. And God created man in his own image as the last of his creation commanding man to have dominion over every of his creation. The likeness that God create man in his likeness is the intellect. God is the intelligence that bring life and God create man in the likeness of his intelligence to dominate life and not physical likeness as many people assume.

You can see that the evolution theory of Science is similar to the creation story of Moses step by step which make it mean that Science and the Bible are saying the same thing using different words to say it.

THE BEGINNING ACCORDING TO PHILOSOPHY

To Philosophy life originate from a single mind which it call the universal mind and everything originate from the universal mind. Although Philosophy have their division like Science and Religion that have their division.

The universal mind is the mind of the universe that split into many minds that generate each galaxy. The galaxy then give birth to many minds that form so many stars. The stars then generate solar system along with planet earth. In planet earth, life develop from the lowest mind that form a static body to higher mind that form movable body.

From the development of one mind to the other that start from the universal mind, everything shape themselves according to the nature of each mind. From stage to stage, the development of each mind took place up to the development of the human mind that shape itself according to the human body.

Science believe in evolution of the body, Philosophy believe in evolution of the mind but the Bible speak of daily creation. Science believe that life start from the big bang and therefore did not recognize God, Philosophy believe in the universal mind and therefore they are atheist, and Religion believe in God as the creation of life.

Science advocate that in every action there is equal and opposite reaction, Philosophy advocate the law of cause and effect and say in every effect there is a cause and Religion is advocating the law of sowing and reaping, that everyone will reap what they sow. These three principle advocated by Science, Philosophy and Religion are the foundation that life was erected.

THE UNITY

Science, Philosophy, and Religion describe the source of life from the angle that each of them view life from base on the level of the understanding of life by each of them.

If Science say that the beginning of life is a pure energy and Philosophy say that the beginning of life is a universal mind and Religion say the life begin from God, are they not using different language to describe what that is beyond the perceptive capacity of the brain.

If one should ask the scientist to describe this pure energy, the scientist will say that the pure energy is responsible for the big bang but energy cannot generate itself, something must generate it. If one should ask the philosopher to describe the universal mind, the philosopher will say that the universal mind is the intelligence behind creation but there cannot be intelligence without something generating the intelligence. If one should ask the religionist to describe God, the religionist will say that God is what it is but this is not a description.

You can see that Science, Philosophy, and Religion are arguing over what each of them cannot describe and what the three of them are describing are element of the source of life and not the source of life itself.

To Science, life defy a single definition and since Science cannot investigate God nor any form of spirit, it could not believe in God nor any form of spirit. And since scientist can synthesize the body chemistry of man, they could not believe in a God that made man in it image and therefore a God that have human body chemistry because it will mean that the scientist can synthesize the body chemistry of God.

If one is to believe in a creator, one must overlook the saying of the Bible that seem to belittle God and the saying of other holy book that seem to create fantasy on God. To believe in a creator, one must be convince that there is intelligence that create life through personal experience and understand that the intelligence that create life is beyond the perceptive capacity of the brain.

THE DIFFENCE IN RELIGION

As there are difference between Science, Philosophy and Religion, so there are differences in religion group and there difference is base on their different level of the understanding of life.

The atheist see the intelligence that create life from the angle that God cannot be seen and this is a fact for no one can see God which make it seem as if there is no God. The polytheist see God in every god as the manifestation of God and this is true because everything came from God. Some people may argue that they are disobedient angels but if the omniscient God that is all knowledge that is believed to know the future create them, why did it create them knowing that they will become disobedient? As you and I have the free will to do good or evil, so these gods have the free will to do good or evil and this is not a problem to the creator because everything operate in a circle and evil will return to it starting point to destroy the person or the god that bring it forth according to the level of the evil and this is the hell that some religion are trying to describe. The monotheist although cannot see God, see only God and refuse to recognize or accept anything outside God and this is a fact for there is nothing that exist without the will of God.

As we have the hand, the leg, and the anus in one body, so every religion are of one body. Some religion can be compare to the hand, some compare to the leg, and some compare to the anus but the anus smell and it is not of a good sight.

Let the one that believe in God not condemn the one that believe not in God. If anyone believe in God, it did not add anything to God and if anyone did not believe in God, it did not reduce anything from God. If one believe in God and did not live according to the law that govern life, such one will be compared to the anus.

Since there is no one that can see God nor prove to everyone that there is God, there is no one that have the right to condemn the atheist for they are expressing their opinion and everyone is entitle to their opinion, if the opinion is not hostile to life.

It is by saying that my religion is right and your religion is wrong that is causing religion intolerance that have lead to the lost of many life. What evidence do you have that your religion is right and the religion of the other person is wrong. As you have your holy book that support what you say, so the other person have his or her holy book that support what he or she say. Any holy book that support the peaceful existence of life is a book working for life and not against life, therefore there is no one that have the right to condemn it. In the Bible, in Luke chapter 9 verse 49, John was telling Jesus that they saw a man expelling demons by the use of the name of Jesus and they try to prevent the man because he is not following Jesus. In reply, Jesus told them that they should not prevent such person and that he that is not against them is for them. If one holy book is teaching the truth and another holy book is teaching the same truth, they are a book working for the peaceful existence of life, therefore working for the peaceful existence of each other and not against each other.

Every religion refuse to see what cannot be accepted in their holy book but see what that cannot be accepted in another holy book. Jesus walk on water and no one said that Jesus practice magic but a Budhist Lama walk on air and a Christian sect say that the Budhist Lama is practicing magic. Jesus said that if there is a rafter in your eye and you want to remove a speck from the eye of another person, you must first remove the rafter from your eye so that you can see clearly to remove the speck from the other person's eye.

HOW LIFE BEGIN

The law evolve to become a mind that generate the intelligence that created a directed motion that get life started.

The scientist consider the story of the Bible about the source of life called God by religion to be an illusion while the religionist that are in agreement with the Bible consider the theory of evolution to be an illusion which make it seem that Science and Religion are against each other. What they fail to realize is that they are saying the same thing in a different way.

Many things that seem to be illusion seem to be so because they appear to be beyond the perceptive capacity of the brain. Jesus walk on water as recorded by the Bible but everybody did not believe it and metal and plastic put together in a certain way can fly and everybody believe it because they see it fly yet many people did not understand how a metal and plastic put together in a certain way can fly. Because one did not understand the principle of how something work did not make it to be an illusion.

Science say that life is govern by physical and chemical law and life originate from this law and we come out of this law as the apex of it. If life originate from the law that govern physics and chemistry which form the base for the beginning of life, then we can say that God that is beyond the understanding of man is the law that govern physics and chemistry that originate life.

Jesus said that God is a spirit – John chapter 4 verse 24 and also said that the words that he speaks to us are spirit and life – John chapter 6 verse 63. If the word that Jesus teach us is a spirit and it is the law that Jesus teach us, then the law is God that give life because it is only God that can give life.

In the gospel according to John, it begin by saying that in the beginning was the word and the word was with God and the word was God. It went further to say that nothing was made that is in existence without the word. When we look at the word "word", it is an expression of thought for there can never be a word without a thought and there can never be a thought without a mind.

If the word of God can take form and become Christ, the first born of creation, cannot the law take form and become God? In Proverb chapter 8, it describe wisdom and understanding as Christ, the beginning of creation thereby personifying wisdom and understanding.

Jesus said that he is the way and the truth and the life – John chapter 14 verse 6. In chapter 10 of the same John, Jesus said that he is in union with the Father and the Father is in union with him and if we did not believe that he is in union with the Father, we should believe on account of his work. Jesus personify God as his Father because he is the word of God. Philosophy believe that a perfect mind will become one with the universal mind which is similar to Jesus saying that he and God are one.

One may ask that how can the law be God? But Jesus said in John chapter 16 verse 12 that "I have many thing to say to you, but you are not able to bear them at present" and verse 13 say that "However, when the one arrives, the spirit of truth, he will guide you into all truth..." If we look deep into the law, the law is beyond human understanding and it was a bit of the understanding of the law that make technological development to have gone so far. It was the understanding of the law of gravity that make human to build a vehicle that can fly and it was the understanding of the law of either that make human to build a device that can make one person in one continent able to speak with another person in another continent. If human can understand the law, nothing will be impossible for human because the law is life itself.

The pure law is beyond human imagination and it exists by itself. The pure law took form and become a pure energy that split into a pure positive energy and a pure negative energy. It is the coming together of the pure positive energy and the pure negative energy that caused the big bangs that get life started.

The pure positive energy form the world of light where everything is perfection and the pure negative energy form the world of darkness, the world of illusion that nothing exist but illusion. It is the pure positive energy that the Bible call God and it is the pure negative energy that the Bible call the devil for the devil is an illusion of darkness.

Magic, sorcery, the black art and witchcraft are all illusion of darkness for they are not real to anyone that dwell in the light but will be real to anyone that dwell in darkness for the illusion of darkness will make them real. If you strictly live a positive life, magic, sorcery, the black art and witchcraft will not exist for you and you will not exist for them.

The law appear to the Jews in the form of Jehovah and gave them the book of the law through Moses. The law appear to the Hindu in the form of Krshna and gave them the book of the law through Arjuna. The law appear to Mohammed in a cave through a messenger called Angel Gabriel and speak the Holy Quran to him.

Anywhere people observe the law whether in the name of Science, Philosophy or Religion, they are worshipping the creator, the source of life.

The issue of God is a sensitive issue that depend on individual understanding. Each person can only experience God in a personal way and it is difficult for one person to prove this experience to another person for it is a personal experience that can be difficult to use words to describe.

My late paternal grandmother, late Madam Ekeneme Emzana was the priestess of a god in my home town, Irri, Delta State, Nigeria. The name of her god is Ẹtẹredhedhẹ. As a teenager, I use to go to her shrine not to worship her god but to spend some time with her as a grandson to a grandmother. I experience a lot of things from her that is beyond explanation about the reality of her god. To an outsider, the god may not be real but to an insider that have spend some time with her will know that the god is real. One day, I was in her shrine, someone that newly die in my home town came to her shrine and my grandmother was asking this newly dead person what the person was doing in her shrine, that when the person was alive, the person don't visit her shrine. This experience stay with me for a long time that dead people are still alive and I cannot prove this to another person.

My late uncle, Engr. Monday Emezana and his friend went to a swamp in a distance forest in my home town for fishing. They miss their way in the forest until night and in the night, they could not find their way out of the forest. A god brought a light to them and they follow the light and the light lead them out of the forest before the light vanish.

If you don't want to believe in my grandmother and her god or you don't want to believe in the story that a god lead my late uncle and his friend out of the forest, ignore the story because there are many things in life that are difficult to believe.

THE

DEVIL

A

NEGATIVE

FORCE

2

Each person is tempted when he is lured and enticed by his own desire – Saint James

THE ORIGIN OF THE DEVIL

After the splitting of the positive energy and the negative energy from the pure energy, the positive energy and the negative energy repel each other to a distance that is beyond the imagination of anyone.

The positive energy form paradise, the abode of the blessed and the negative energy form hell, the abode of destruction which make heaven and hell to be opposite in extreme to each other.

Hell is not a place that fire burn for eternity as many assume because of the illustration given by Jesus. Hell is a place of eternal destruction, a place for the destruction of evil human soul and every evil spirit.

Jesus said that, "do not be afraid of the one that can destroy the body, be afraid of the one that can destroy the body and soul. It is only God that can destroy the soul, there is no other being, no matter how powerful the being is that have the power to destroy a soul. It is only God that create a soul and it is only God that can destroy it.

After the creation of the world of light by the positive energy and the world of darkness by the negative energy, other world lower than the pure world of light start taking form.

The world of light is a world of perfection where everything is perfect and it is called heaven by the religionist. Other world that are less in perfection were taking form with the next one less and less in perfection up to a point. The world of darkness formed by the negative force is a place of perpetual darkness, a place where everything is nothing. The world of illusion where everything that exist is an illusion. Other world that were less in darkness start taking form and world after world that were less and less in darkness start emerging. World after world that were less and less in darkness and illusion with a better form were taking form. It is the midpoint where the creation by the negative energy meet with the creation by the positive energy that combine to create this our world, a place where good and evil exist side by side, a world of duality.

Outside the earth world and everything related to the earth world, evil have it place and good have it place and the two have no form of contact. Jesus use it in the parable of Lazarus and the rich man when he said that after the death of Lazarus and the rich man, both of them have no form of contact.

To confirm that the world of light exist, the Bhagavad gita speak of Krshna to be the creator of life, the Bible speak of Jehovah to be the creator of life and the Quran speak of Allah to be the creator of life. Jehovah said in the

Bible, "let us create man in our image and likeness". Who was Jehovah speaking to? In the Holy Holy Quran, it was said that, "we empower Jesus with the Holy Spirit". Who are these 'we"? These confirm the reality of the world of light.

Everything in the world of light operate at the speed of light, that is one of the reason we cannot see any being that appear on earth for a purpose except if they show themselves to us. Their movement is within the range of the speed of light. The human eyes cannot catch up with the speed of light and the texture of light is too fine that human eyes cannot see it and it is too bright that it will blind the human eyes. This is the reason that Jehovah said to Moses in Mount Sinai that no one can see him and live. The bacteria and the virus have been in existence since the beginning of time but they are too small that the human eyes cannot see them except by the aid of an instrument.

Can we believe the Bhagavad gita, can we believe the Holy Bible, can we believe the Holy Quran. The only prove that I have that can make us believe in them is the moral truth that they teach us for if we live by their moral truth, life will be good and easy for us but if we neglect to live by their moral truth, life will be hard and difficult for us.

The point where material creation start from is the point where the pure positive energy meet with the pure negative energy. The creation of everything in the material world result from the coming together of the positive energy with the negative energy which is why you will see that everything material is the combination of the positive and the negative. The atom which is the smallest material unit have a negative charged electron and a positive charged proton which is an example of the combination of the positive energy and the negative energy at the lowest material unit.

The coming together of the positive energy and the negative energy create the human body and it is after the creation of the material body that the spirit which is associated with the mind that animate the human body descend into the human body. If there is no spirit that animate the body, the human body will have not taste death because death is the separation of the spirit that animate the body from the body.

With the creation of human, human is suppose to repel the negative energy of the darkness which is part of his or her body just as the positive repel the negative and be fit to dwell in paradise, the abode of the most high, the perfect city of God where everything is perfection.

A religion sect believe that man was created out of the waste product after creating angels which is the reason for the imperfection of human while another religion believe that the soul of plant develop to the soul of animal and the soul of animal develop to the soul of man and the soul of man have to develop to the soul of angel and be fit to live in paradise while some sect believe that the soul will become one with God. Anyone that you believe in, or if your religion believe in something different, the end result is for human to be fit to live a peaceful eternal life.

If you believe that when you die all will end for you, death will give you the result when you die whether all will end for you or not because everyone will taste death one day.

Religion believe in paradise, the perfect place that every good soul will go after their death and some believe that it is after judgement day. The peaceful atheist Budhist believe in nirvana, a state of blissful peace, a form of paradise. Philosophy believe that a perfect mind will become one with the universal mind, another form of paradise. Science did not believe in paradise because it cannot believe in what that cannot be prove with test tube or any scientific equipment and paradise is beyond test tube or any scientific equipment.

Paradise is not a place of inactivity as many people assume. Paradise is a place of joyful peaceful activities. Jesus said in Matthew chapter 11 verse 11 that "of anyone born by a woman, there is no one greater than John the Baptist but the least person in the Kingdom of God is greater than John the Baptist" which mean that paradise is a place for great people, people that are great in mental strength.

Eckarkar say that we will become a co-worker with God and before anyone can work with God, the person's level of spiritual development must be at the level of paradise, the region of light that have no form of darkness.

Many people think that by becoming part of a religion will earn them the right to gain entry to paradise. There is no religion that can earn anyone the right to dwell in paradise. It is the maturity of anyone to perfection that will earn one the right to dwell in paradise that is why Jesus said that many are called but few are chosen. The perfection is not material perfection it is mental perfection which is the ability to have a clean mind, a perfect mind that don't think any form of evil.

Paradise is the highest height, although a religion sect believe that there is always one step ahead.

The deepest depth is a place of absolute darkness as the highest height is a place of absolute light. The deepest depth is a place of eternal death where a soul will be destroyed forever while the highest height is a place of eternal life where a soul will live forever.

The deepest depth is a place of absolute darkness, a state of nothing and any soul that descend to the deepest depth will become nothing, will cease to exist and before any soul will descend to the deepest depth, the soul will pass through stages of severe pain. The lower a soul descend to the dark world, the more severe the pain will be, a pain that is beyond the imagination of anyone before the soul get to the point of eternal death.

In the highest world, it is only good mental perfect soul that can dwell there and in the lower world, it is only evil soul that can dwell there that are passing through the process of destruction.

Between the highest world the world of light and the deepest world the world of darkness lie many world with the earth world where light and darkness dwell side by side as the middle point.

Every soul will die to the world that match his or her level of good or evil which are his or her level of light or darkness. Apostle Paul mention the stages of the higher world when he said in second Corinthians chapter 12 verse 2 to 4 that he saw a man in union with Christ fourteen years ago that was caught up to the third heaven. Apostle Paul also recognize the lower world by saying in Roman chapter 10 verse 6 to 7 that who will ascend to heaven and bring Christ down or who will descend to the deep and bring Christ up from the dead because the deepest world is a place for the dead. By saying this, Apostle Paul recognize the earth as the midpoint and the deep, the world of darkness, a place for the dead, a place that an evil soul will be destroyed to eternal death and some religion see the lower world as the hellish world.

THE BELIEVE IN THE DEVIL

To the atheist and the polytheist, the devil did not exist. It is the monotheist that is advocating the devil with the believe that the devil is fighting against the people of God, therefore against God.

The monotheist personify the devil as they personify God. To Philosophy, the devil did not exist but believe in the existence of a negative force, a force that propel one to do evil. Science cannot believe in what that cannot be prove, so it did not concern itself with the devil.

The believe in the devil and the believe that the devil is fighting against the people of God, therefore against God put doubt in the mind of zealot people about the supremacy of God. It make them assume that if the devil is fighting against the people of God make the devil to be nearly if not equal in strength with God since God is doing nothing about it now but postpone it to the future. If one fight against another by destroying what belong to the other without the other doing anything about it at the time of the destruction show a type of fear.

The question that always come to the mind of intelligent people concerning the devil is that if God is omniscient, knowing everything, why did God create the devil knowing that the devil will fight against him by fighting against his creation. If I know that if I give birth to a child that will bring destruction to the world, I will not marry and if I marry, I will not bear a child. The issue of the devil and God bring doubt to the mind of many people concerning the supremacy of God, it make some people to doubt if God is real and also make some people not to believe in God.

God is beyond perfection. God is omnipresent, omniscient, and omnipotent, meaning that God is everywhere at the same time, and God is all power and all knowledge.

The story of the garden of Eden make the devil to appear petty and it defy God putting God at the level of human. Although the world have not advance in knowledge at the time of penning the story of the garden of Eden and the story was written for the people of the era of Moses and not for this our modern era which the story appear bizarre to.

The Bible is written by inspiration, including every other holy book and Apostle Paul confirm it by saying that all scripture are inspired by God, although there are verses that are claim to be dictated like the ten commandments and other laws that was given through Moses.

If one get a message from God through inspiration or if it is dictated to one by a higher being, one may forget some part of it due to anxiety and in order to pen the whole of it down, one may assume what was forgotten and write it along which will make it to deviate from the original. This was recognize in Deuteronomy chapter 18 verse 22 when God said that if a prophet speak in the name of God and the word did not come true, that is the word that God did not speak, with presumption the prophet spoke it. Some religion stories are exaggerated presumption and some are illustration like Jesus Christ that sometime speak in illustration and explain the meaning to his disciples.

THE PURPOSE OF THE DEVIL

The existence of the devil is different from the way the monotheist religion imagines the devil to be. Philosophy is correct by describing the devil as a negative force, a force that propel one to do evil. Everything in life is created for a purpose and the devil is not an exception.

The devil was created out of darkness and darkness is an illusion, it only seem to exist because we cannot see through it which make the devil to be an illusion.

At the highest height is the positive energy which is the light and this light manifest as God and the Bible say that God is light and Science see this light as a pure energy.

When Moses return from the top of mount Sinai, where he went to meet God, his face was radiating light, an emission from God.

At the deepest depth is the negative energy which manifest as the darkness that the devil spring from which is the illusion of darkness. It is from worldly plane down to a certain dept that the darkness took form and the form it take is a negative force which manifest from the negative energy.

The negative force serve as the downward pull of the mind to the illusion of materialism. Everything material have a force of attraction due to the negative force and everything material are transient which make materialism to be a form of illusion that deceive people that succumb to them to evil. The love of materialism, including the love of beauty of the nude make the darkness to attract every stray human to destruction by it.

The positive force serve as the upward pull of the mind to God which is the reason of human innate of searching for God, the source f life.

The way to the perfect city where everything is perfection is to overcome the negative force which serve as the downward pull of the mind to materialism and to overcome this force is not an easy task. Everyone must overcome this force if one desire to live a good life and it is living a good life that lead to the perfect city of God where everything is perfection.

Without the negative force that have a downward pull of the mind to materialism and the positive force that counter it by having an upward pull of the mind to God, human will not live a life of a choice but will be like a programme robot that did not have a life of it own. Angel have a life of their own because they are a matured being that did not have any form of negativity because the light in them always dispel every form of darkness that come close to them for darkness can never come near the light.

Consider if your child do things base on your reason alone without attaching any of his or her own reason to anything he or she do. The child will appear like a dummy to you and will not grow to be a responsible adult. Will you want such child?

Human can be compared to a raw gold that have to pass through a red hot fire before they can glow and the purpose of the devil is to make human pass through this red hot fire through the pull of the mind to materialism so that the positive in human can come forth and glow after passing through many pain due to ignorant.

The devil was created out of darkness and when you enter a dark place and bring light to the dark place, the light will dispel the darkness and what you will see is nothing for the darkness is an illusion.

If you bring light to your life by living a positive life, every form of darkness which belong to evil will vanish from your life but if you did not live a positive life, the darkness will take control of your life through pain and hardship.

Whether one believe the story of the Garden of Eden to be true or to be myth, it serve to describe the purpose the devil was created for and the purpose is to lead the mentally strong to God and lead the mentally weak to itself to cease to become personal and become nothing.

THE LESSON OF THE GARDEN OF EDEN

The story of the Garden of Eden say that God created the Garden of Eden with different fruit bearing trees and plant a tree with the fruit of knowledge in the midst of the garden, a fruit that will make anyone that eat it to know good and evil.

God created human and place human in the Garden of Eden and command human to eat from any fruit of any tree in the garden except from the fruit of the tree of knowledge.

Human was living in the Garden of Eden walking about naked in an ignorant state. Satan the devil came to Eve and tell Eve that if they eat from the fruit of the tree of knowledge, they will become knowing like God, they will know good and evil and they will become like God.

The story was written in figure of speech and my explanation of the story is that Satan the devil was not happy with the way Adam and Eve were walking about naked and living in ignorant in the Garden of Eden. Satan the devil introduce Eve and Adam to knowledge that Eve and Adam can know what is good and what is evil.

Knowledge is constructive and it is also destructive and according to the story, it is the destructive side of knowledge that God was hiding from human. The good side of knowledge cannot only be known, knowing the good side of knowledge always comes along with knowing the evil side of knowledge. Everything that have a good purpose also have an evil purpose.

If you were in the position of Adam and Eve, will you prefer to live forever and walk about naked in an ignorant state or you will succumb to the temptation of Satan the devil and live a good life for a short period of time. I rephrase the question, will you prefer to live under trees and cave forever or you will prefer to live for a short period of time in a beautiful building with the latest facilities? Every choice you choose has it good side and bad side but I will prefer to live a good life for a short period of time than to live all my life in ignorant state forever.

The negative force called the devil is working for God but Religion believe that the devil is working against God.

Let us assume that if the story of the Garden of Eden is not in figure of speech. If Adam and Eve did not succumb to Satan the devil, we will all be walking about naked in an ignorant state in good health forever. Adam and Eve succumb to Satan the devil and we are all enjoying evolving technological development but living for a short period of time.

Desire is the base for temptation but to be tempted depend on the type of life you are living. If you are living a negative life, everything you desire will lead you to negativity and will lead you to the life of illusion.

The only way you will never connect to the negative force is to strictly control your mind against any form of negativity. Strictly control your mind to live a positive life and do not allow any form of negativity to dwell in your mind.

When one desire something, one will get connected either to the positive force to get the thing positively or to the negative force to get the thing negatively and whichever one dwell upon is what that will take the control of the mind. The positive force and the negative force are what make you and me a human being and angel are the being that their positive force always repel the negative force and all human can attain this point which will earn them the right to live in the perfect city of God where everything is perfection.

It is the force that we gave our attention to that will take the control of our mind and repel the other for the two forces cannot dwell in our mind at the same time, it is either one or the other.

The positive force work to draw the mind to perfection and the negative force work to give strength to those that succumb to the positive force to help to draw the mind to perfection through trial and temptation and work for the destruction of those that succumb to the negative force.

The purpose of the negative force called the devil is to give anyone the ticket to enter the perfect city where everything is perfection through trial and temptation brought upon oneself through what one desire and few are the people that can pass through the negative force called the devil.

The negative force is merciless in it mission which make the monotheist to think that the devil is fighting against the work of God, therefore against God.

Many religionist wait patiently for their dying day so that death can warrant them the ticket to the perfect kingdom of God. What they forget to realize is that today must be successful before tomorrow can be successful because it is the way we live our life today that will determine our tomorrow.

If one cannot live a successful life today, there is no possibility that one can live in a successful heaven tomorrow for it is the present that determine the future.

Whether one is rich or not, if one is not living a successful earth life, one cannot live in a successful peaceful heaven. Successful earth life depend on how you live with yourself which depend on the organization of your mind, how you live with your family members and how you live with your environment and when combine together will determine the type of life you are living.

The meaning of the words devil, hell, and many other words in every holy book can be due to language barrier and some are metaphor. In every language, there are some words that are difficult to translate to another language and when translated to another language may give a different meaning. For example, in the Yoruba language in Nigeria, when someone come back home, the person at home will greet the person that come back home "ẹkuabọ" meaning welcome and the one that come back home will greet the one at home "ẹkuile". The Yoruba word "ẹkuile" cannot be translated to any other language. The English language word "quarrel" cannot be translated to the Yoruba language and if it is translated will give a different meaning from the English language word "quarrel".

GOOD

AND

EVIL

3

No one can serve two masters, he will either hate one and love the other or be devoted to one and despise the other – Jesus

THE WORLD OF DUALITY

Without good, life will not have existed till today because people in the world will have destroyed themselves.

Good is the word that describe something that we are in agreement with and the word "God" was coin out of the word "good". Evil is the word that describes something that we are not in agreement with and the word "devil" was coin out of the word "evil".

If there is no hot, we will not realize the important of cold and if there is no cold, we will not realize the important of hot. Hot and cold exist side by side to complement each other.

There is the male and there is the female. Without the male, there will not be the female and the male cannot exist without the female. The male and the female exist side by side to complement each other.

An atom have a positive charged proton and a negative charged electron and it is the force of attraction between the positive charged proton and the negative charged electron that make the atom to exist as a unit. If the negative charged electron refused to harmonize with the positive charged proton, life will cease to exist because the atom is the tangible unit of life. Electricity was derived from separating the negative charged electron from the positive charged proton, using it to run every electrical device. If the negative charged electron refused to complement the positive charged proton, technological development will not have gone so far.

There is the wet season and there is the dry season. The wet season is meant for the planting of crops and the dry season is meant for harvesting and the two seasons cannot do without each other for the existence of the cultivation of crops.

Life exist on earth because of the nature of it duality and the dual nature of life make us to realize the importance of the opposite.

If you did not understand the dual nature of life, you will condemn one nature over the other nature but the fact remain the same, one nature cannot exist without the other nature.

The dual nature of life make it seem as if one nature is fighting against the other nature but it duality is aiding the existence of each other.

A lot of people think that evil is fighting against good but without evil we will not realize the important of good, like the people that have experience war will realize the importance of peace. Will one then say that life created evil for we human so that we can realize the importance of good? This is not the case because evil is the absent of good just like darkness that is the absent of light.

If you live positive, you are living by the positive force called God and if you live negative, you are living by the negative force called the devil and whichever you embrace will take the control of your life.

Anytime you do something that is evil, you are adding strength to the negative force to take the control of more of your life and to reign as king over you. Anytime you do something that is good, you are adding strength to the positive force to take the control of more of your life and to reign as king over you.

When a person commit a bad act, the person may blame the act on evil and it source and say that the devil lead him or her to it but it is our desire that lead to the temptation the we face and to resist temptation depend on out mental strength to resist the temptation.

Some people may say that they are deceived forgetting that everyone have the choice to do good or evil which depend on the one that we give our attention to. In James chapter 1 verse 14, Apostle James said that each one is tempted when he is enticed by his own desire. In the story of the Garden of Eden, Eve said that was the serpent that deceived her but Eve was enticed to the fruit. The serpent did not deceive Eve to eat the fruit, it only suggest to Eve the reason to eat the fruit and it is left to Eve to accept the reason or reject it.

We are created with the will power to act or not to act base on our intellect which is the ability to think before we make a choice to act or not act. It is this that differentiate human from animal that act base on impulse.

God is light and the devil is darkness. If you dwell in good, you will dwell in the light and you will dwell in God and the light will light your path and brighten everything you do. If you dwell in evil, you will dwell in darkness and be of the devil and your path will become dark and this darkness will darken everything that you do and everything that belong to you.

Light and darkness can never mix because darkness is the absent of light. If you want darkness to leave your life, you don't have to pursue it, all you have to do is to bring light to your life by living a positive life and the darkness will flee by itself.

In James chapter 2 verse 10, Apostle James said that whoever keep the whole law and fail in one point have become accountable to all of it. For the light of God to dwell in your life, you must strictly live in accord with the law that govern life.

When you start keeping the law that govern life, you may not see changes immediately but if you persist, with time, you will start seeing changes. The reason you will not see immediate changes is that when you start moving away from darkness by living a positive life, you will start moving away from the darkness that bind you one step at a time because you are not experience in keeping all the law that govern life. You will keep some and you will break some. You will break some by mistake and others due to attraction of the negative force and not until you keep the whole law that govern life that the light will brighten your path and everything you do.

You will apply the whole of the law that govern life bit by bit till you will develop the inner strength to live by them if you persist to live by them in your daily life.

Everyone have a nature that is good which is of the light and also a nature that is evil which is of the darkness and it is the one that we allow to dwell inside us that will take the control of our mind.

Your body may want you to take to an act, for instance, to have an illicit sex. If your inner growth is toward the light, you will overcome the want but if your inner growth is toward the darkness, the want will overcome you and you will not stop till you have the illicit sex.

You may have many questions in your mind that need answers. The more you inwardly grow to the light, the more you will have answers to your questions reveal to you and the answers to many things in life will become known to you. But if your inner growth is toward the darkness and if the answers to your questions are laid directly before you, you will not know it nor understand it. This is why Jesus said that seeing, they do not see and hearing, they do not hear, even though they have eyes to see and ears to hear.

A lot of people believe in God and some group of people did not believe in God. If you are among the group that did not believe in God, do not worry, keep doing good and God will be there for you, for the issue of God is a personal experience.

God is omnipresent. God will be everywhere for you if you keep doing good and God will be nowhere for you if you keep doing evil.

PART 2

THE

ACT

OF

LIFE

THE

PATH

TO

THE

LIGHT

4

The Lord guide the path of the righteous and the holy ones – King David

THE RIGHT THINGS

To some people, the right thing is to live a moral life and to some other people, the right thing is to be righteous. But the right thing in life is the combination of living a moral life and living a righteous life.

It is possible for anyone to decide to live a moral life and start living it immediately but it is not possible for anyone to decide to do the right thing and start living it immediately because it take persistence practice to know how to do the right thing always. To speak the right words depend on your experience of using the right words.

Knowing when to speak and when not to speak, knowing what to say and the right time to say it and knowing what not to say depend on your experience with people on how they react to what they hear and when they hear it.

Living the right life depend on how you relate with different people which have much to do with your experience in human relation. If you are not experience in human relation and on how human act and react, you may misunderstand people and those that are not experience may misunderstand you and misunderstanding each other can lead to a chaotic condition.

Consider the way Jesus handle the case of a woman that was brought to him that she was caught in the act of adultery and according to the Jewish law, anyone caught in the act of adultery is to be stone to death. If Jesus tell them to leave the woman, it will bring disagreement between Jesus and the people because of the law and that may not change the woman. Jesus put the situation under control by saying that the person that have never commit a sin since the person was born should be the first person to throw the first stone at the woman. The people left one by one from the eldest to the youngest to remain Jesus and the woman and Jesus command the woman to stop living a sinful life. If Jesus was not diplomatic with the issue, it could have lead to a chaotic condition.

Living the right life is like a child learning to walk and as there is no child that can learn to walk in one day, so there is no one that can start living the right life in one day.

As a child have to learn to stand and balance himself or herself first before lifting the first step, so everyone must first know what is right before doing what is right.

When a child lift the first step to the second step to the third step, falling always accompany it but the child never get discourage. When one know what is right, the first attempt to do what is right is often difficult but with further attempt to do what is right, it become easy. If doing the right thing is difficult for you, do not be discourage, keep on trying to do what is right and with time, to do what is right will become easy for you.

What motivate the child to try again after every failed attempt? The motivation come from the people that the child see walking which always put the desire in the child to learn to walk. Suppose adult don't walk, children will not think of learning to walk, so also is doing the right thing.

Jesus said that for anyone to enter the kingdom of God, such one must become like a little child because the little child never get discourage in learning the basic things of life. Everyone must never get discourage in learning to live the right life even if it seem hard to live the right life.

MOTIVATION

As a child get motivation by seeing adult walking, so everyone get motivation by seeing what other people do to do what they do.

The mind is like a camera that record everything that pass through it view point and start replaying when the mind is idle which give some type of motivation in a certain way which make it important to command our attention.

Be strict with what you allow your eyes to see and your ears to hear so that they don't give you negative motivation to act in a certain way when you are in a state of anxiety. When anyone is in a state of anxiety, the person will act base on what was stored in the person's mind whether consciously or unconsciously without looking to reason whether the person realize it or not.

Anxiety is an emotional state and when you are in an emotional state, you may not remember to look to reason if the emotion have taking the control of your mind. For example, the emotion of anger can make a gentle person to fight if the gentle person allow the emotion of anger to take the control of his or her mind. Jesus said that we must not be anxious of tomorrow because of the nature of anxiety to cloud reason.

As a child get motivation to walk again after each failed attempt by seeing people walking, so everyone will get motivation to live the right life after each failed attempt to live the right life by seeing people living the right life or reading books that inspire to live the right life. But after each failed attempt to live the right life if there are no people that are living the right life or if there is no book that inspire people to live the right life, one may become tired of learning to live the right life and one may drop from trying to live the right life.

As you start practicing to live the right life, you must avoid people that are living the wrong life because if you mix with people that are living a wrong life, they will make you to live a wrong life.

For you to live the right life you must associate only with people that are living the right life and avoid people that are living the wrong life because the company that you keep will determine your character.

LIVING THE RIGHT LIFE

Living the right life depend on our understanding of life and the angle that we view life from.

If anyone view life from the negative side of life, it will be difficult for this type of person to live the right life for living the right life strictly depend on living a positive life and viewing life from the positive side of life.

To live the right life, you must be tolerant for if you find it difficult to tolerate people, people will also find it difficult to tolerate you. Tolerance begins from the mind. If you always think of the past wrong that someone have done, you will find it difficult to tolerate people because thinking of the past wrong always lead to intolerance.

To live the right life, you must be patient with everyone and everything. Some people are always in a hurry because they don't want to waste time nor can they afford to be patient with people. They always want everything done before time or at the nick of time. There is nothing wrong to want to do things on time or at the nick of time but when it become an obsession, it will become a problem to the person.

When one is too fast, one may miss some important point. As it is not good to be slow, it is not good to be too fast if one cannot control his or her speed, what everyone have to do is to keep pace with time.

To live the right life, you should endure any situation you cannot change. Any situation you cannot change will change itself with the passing of time. After reading this, one may say to himself or herself that he or she will endure everyone or any situation but there is no one that can endure more than his or her endurance limit. If you know that the level of your endurance is low, work on it and makes it high by practising to endure everyone and everything in your mind. If you practice endurance mentally, you will be able to endure physically for it is the level of endurance that separates the master from the student.

When Jesus was tried before the ruling council, Jesus maintain perfect silence without defending himself and when death sentence was place on him, he did not accuse anyone, this is the peak of endurance. Everyone should strive to attain the highest limit of endurance, although it takes time and a persistence practice for anyone to achieve.

To live the right life, one should be content. Contentment start from the mind and the eyes are the window of the mind. If you did not live a dual life that see one thing to be beautiful and the other to be ugly for everything in life have their own form of beauty and you did not see one thing to be much and the other to be little, you will not have problem with contentment.

To live the right life, one must be calm for calmness is the chief of all virtue that make the practice of every other virtue to be easy. If you can become calm, you will clearly see your way through life and to live the right life will be an easy thing for you.

If you can become calm, your brain will release endorphin, a substance that will make you feel good and look young by rejuvenating your body cells and give you a youthful vigor. If your mind is troubled, your brain will release stress hormone which will make you loose vigor and age your body cells which will make you look old.

To be calm is to remove every thought from your mind both positive and negative thought which will make you remain calm and to continue in calmness, you are to dwell in mental silence and remain inwardly quiet.

To live the right life, you are to develop the strength to meet your daily activities. Laziness depends on the way you are living your life. If you are living a debase life, it will take away your strength and you may become lazy. Living a debase life or dwelling in negative thought will make your brain release stress hormone that will be making you become tired.

To live the right life, you are to avoid becoming greedy. Greedy people are restless people and you need peace of mind in order to live the right life. If you are greedy, what the greed will take away from you will be more than what you will get by the greed. Greed attract enemy and it destroy every good association.

To live the right life, you are to avoid anger because anger is an emotional state that easily take the control of the mind negatively. If you let anger to take the control of your mind, you will say things that you will not say when you are calm and you may speak what others will hold against you.

If you allow yourself to become angry, your mind will start controlling you instead of you to control your mind. If you allow your mind to control you, it is every negative things that are stored in your mind that will come forth but if you control your mind, it is every positive things that are stored in your mind that you will bring forth. In everything you do, if you always control your mind, you will become successful but if you allow your mind to control you through anger, you will be destroying your own success by your own hands.

To live the right life, you have to avoid jealousy nor should you do anything that will make anyone jealous. If you make people jealous, they will wish you bad luck and it will have effect on you or not base on your psychic condition. When you are angry or jealous, your immune system will become depress and if your immune system become depress, it will become weak to resist infection.

To live the right life, you must not harbor fear. Fear are of two type: a positive fear which is protective and a negative fear which is destructive.
Positive fear is when you are afraid of jumping from the top of a building or when you are afraid of something that is destructive to life which make positive fear to preserve life. Negative fear is when you are afraid of doing what you are suppose to do because you are afraid of the result that it will bring whether it will be a failure.

As positive fear preserve life, negative fear destroyed life. If you are afraid of what you are suppose to do because you are afraid that you may fail in it, you are destroying your own life. If you do something positive and you fail in it, you are suppose to learn the reason behind your failure which suppose to lead to success the next time you do the same thing or will add more knowledge to your knowledge. But when you are afraid to do it the next time because you fail in it your previous time without learning the reason behind the failure, you have mark yourself as a failure.

Negative fear is a great obstacle to life and many people are afraid of the unknown which always prevent them to try their potential. Anybody that is afraid of the unknown will not be able to do much in his or her life because the fear of the unknown will always sap his or her energy. If you are afraid of anything and the doing of the thing, analyze the reason behind the fear to see if the fear is genuine. And if the reason behind the fear is genuine, analyze what it will cost you if you do it and what it will cost you if do not do it and decide which to follow.

To live the right life, you have to banish doubt from your mind because doubt is associated with fear and many time doubt lead to fear. Doubt and fear always go hand in hand and there is no one that can command much energy when in doubt or in fear. If you are in doubt, look within you to see the reason behind the doubt and work on the reason so that the doubt don't create obstacle for you. Find out if your doubt is associated with your former experience or if it is associated with the past or present experience of another person.

To live the right life, you have to avoid the temptation of pride. It is an immature person that will be proud of any achievement. We should know that any achievement that we achieve, someone else can achieve more and if we are proud of any achievement, we are deceiving ourselves. If you are proud of any success, it will be difficult to go beyond the level of the success because the pride will cloud the sense of going beyond the level of the present success.

To live the right life, you must avoid procrastination with all your mental strength because procrastination is associated with a lazy chaotic mind.

If you postpone what you are suppose to do this moment till the next moment, what you are suppose to do this moment will add to what you are going to do the next moment. If you continue to procrastinate, your life will be out of order and can become chaotic.

Put everything you have to do in plan and schedule and follow them through. Anything you are suppose to do this moment, do not wait till the next moment, even if you do not have anything to do the next moment. Put your life in order and do not overlook anything, let everything be important to you.

CULTIVATING A SPIRIT TO BECOME YOU

Everything you do will become alive in you and enhance you to be more of it. The more you do a thing, the more it will become part of you. If you continue to do a thing, it will get to a point that it will become you and if you refuse it to become you, it will become a spirit within you that will be controlling you against your will.

As the mind have effect on the body, so the body has effect on the mind. It is the organ system that we use to carry out the activities of the body influence by the nutrition that we eat that give energy to the organ system of the body to carry out the organ activities that influence the mind to direct the use of the organ for the particular purpose.

If you refuse to nourish your body with a particular nutrition, the organ system that benefit from the nutrition will become weak and it weakness will not influence the mind to use the organ for the behavior that is associated with the organ.

Mystic and priest that practice celibacy don't eat food that raise the level of testorone, a hormone that raise libido which make their mind not to have a strong desire for sex that is beyond their control.

Medical scientist use drug to weak a particular organ by the elimination of the nutrition that the organ benefit from which make the organ to become weak which influence the mind to change toward the behavior that is associated with the organ. Example of this is the drug that is use to calm extremely hostile people by targeting certain brain cell that control hostility. The best method is to use nutrition for there are certain food that can calm the body which have effect on the mind by calming it but sometime food is not effective in controlling a particular behavior especially when the behavior have taken root in the mind.

Every negative behavior is associated with the darkness, the negative force and with the presence of the light, the positive force, the darkness will disappear.

If there is a behavior in you that you do not want, it is your thought that is animating the behavior with life and it is the way you are living your life that is influencing your thought. To change your behavior, the first thing you are to do is to change the way you are living your life, if you are living negative which is having effect on your thought.

If you can change the way you are living your life, it will be easy for you to change the thought that is animating the behavior with life in your mind. For example, if you love too much sleep, it will attract the thought of procrastination to you that will make you to procrastinate. For you to stop procrastination in your life, you will have to remove the thought of procrastination from your mind and for you to remove the thought of procrastination from your mind, you have to sleep only when you are suppose to sleep because to you, it is too much sleep that is the point of the attraction of the thought of procrastination.

If you can live a positive life, your mind will stop to attract negative thought to you which will cut off the supply of negative energy to you that is animating negative behavior with life in you.

There are hypnotic behavior when you are hypnotize with a thought to influence a behavior in you. This is associated with a psychic attack and if you strictly dwell in the light, there is no form of psychic attack that will have effect on you for the present of light will make the darkness not to have any effect

As every living thing need food as energy to stay alive, so every behavior need the thought of the behavior as an energy to stay alive in you. If you are a positive person, it is because you feed your mind with positive thought which influence you to be a positive person and if you are a negative person, it is because you feed your mind with negative thought which influence you to be a negative person. Your mind will feed from what you allow yourself to see, and what you allow yourself to hear, especially the type of programme that you allow yourself to watch on the television and radio and the type of video that you allow yourself to watch on the screen.

Any thought that you feed your mind with continuously is what you will become and that is what will be alive within you and it will become you.

The more you do a thing, the more it will be alive in you and the more it will become you. The more you don't do a thing, the more it will loose it grip on you and as you continue to resist it in your thought, the grip of it on you will become loose if you persist long enough.

As everyone eat good food everyday to stay alive, so you must feed your mind everyday with positive thought for you to remain a positive person. If you don't continuously feed your mind with positive thought by mixing with positive people and avoiding negative people plus reading positive books at your free time, your mind will feed from what it see in your environment and if what you see in your environment is negative, the negativity will influence your mind and you will become a negative person.

Everybody is a combination of the positive and the negative and it is the one that you feed with it own energy that will stay alive in you. If you continuously watch negative scene or negative movie, the scene and movie that use abusive language, quarrel and fighting, you are feeding your mind with negativity and giving energy to negativity to stay alive in you. Look at the society today and how it is filled with negative activities which is making negativity to dominate the mind of people which make negativity to dominate the world.

The mind cannot be a vacuum, it is either you feed it with positive thought by being around positive people and reading positive books or your mind will feed from the negativity that is dominant in your society.

You have to consciously make positive thought dwell in your mind or the negative thought that is dominant in your society will unconsciously dwell in your mind.

Reading a holy book, reading a good book at your free time, listening to a good inspirational speaker from time to time, an inspirational speaker that will influence you to live the right life and avoiding negative people are effort that you will exert for the positive to dwell in you. If you do these continuously for a period of time, the positive will register in your consciousness and you will become a positive person.

When you become a positive person, there is tendency to become a negative person if you did not guard your mind against negativity because it is the negative that dominate the world and have force of attraction than the positive.

If you do not exert effort to remain positive after you have become positive; negativity will silently creep into your mind without your notice till it will take the control of your mind.

Thought are subtle. When a thought enter your mind, it will creep like a thief without your notice till it take the control of your mind.

When King David saw the beautiful nude of Uriah's wife by chance from the top of his building when Uriah's wife was taking her birth. The thought of the beautiful nakedness of Uriah's wife grow in the mind of King David that have the fear of God that the thought of Uriah's wife displace the fear of God in King David mind that the thought of Uriah's wife took over the mind of King David that he end up committing adultery. After committing the adultery, thought of fear that what he have done will become expose, he planted murder.

Negative thought are so powerful that it can corrupt a godly person to act in a stupid way especially when it have to so with the thought of sex, greed, and jealousy.

If you by chance enter a place where a handsome man is having sex with a beautiful woman and you move away immediately, you will see a glimpse of it. If you did not remove what you saw from your mind by not giving it a second thought, the thought will start growing in your mind that will be attracting the desire to have sex with a beautiful person and this desire can grow to the point that it will force you to start having unlawful sex which can lead you to live a debase life to sex.

Anything you see that is negative, you must not allow to register in your mind and this can be done by not giving it a second thought. You can achieve this by becoming personal and not to attach thought to anything that you see or hear.

You must learn not to give your attention to everything that pass through your viewpoint. Some thought can struggle for attention in your mind but you should not resist any thought that struggle for attention because by resisting a thought, you are indirectly giving the thought attention. The way not to give attention to a thought that struggle for your attention is to ignore the thought and divert your mind to another thought that will displace the thought you don't want from your mind or you go into mental silence by not thinking and the thought that struggle for your attention will leave your mind by itself.

Any thought that you continuously think become an act and any act that you continuously do become a habit. If a habit stay with you for a long period of time, it will take the control of your mind and it will become you, it will take form within your mind that will be controlling you against your will. Example of this are smokers that have been expose to the effect of smoking and want to quit smoking but cannot quit because smoking have take form in their mind that is controlling them against their will.

Many people are being control by a type of habit and the common type is the habit of lying. Some people have become one with lying that they lie without any reason for the lie which make them become natural liars. Some may want to speak the truth but because they are one with lying, they end up telling lies.

It is the way that you acquire a habit that you will break away from the habit although it may be difficult to break from a habit that have taken the control of the mind but if one persist long enough, one can break from any habit that have taken the control of the mind.

The way one acquired a habit is through living a negative life which leads to the thought of the habit which leads to the habit. The way to break from a habit is to start living a positive life which will make one have the strength that will enable one to think a positive thought that will displace the negative thought that lead to the habit. If you don't think the thought of a habit, you are cutting the supply of energy to the habit which will make the habit to die away by itself.

The mind and the body have effect on each other and one can be use to control the other.

To use your mind to control your body, direct the mind to the thought of what you want to control about your body and if you persist in holding the thought of what you want to control about the body long enough, your body will yield to the effect of the mind but only if you are living a positive life.

To use your body to control your mind, make your body calm and relax and if you persist long enough, your mind will yield to the effect of your calm body and it will become calm.

There are the position that your body will be that your mind will readily respond to, learn to know these position by experience and learn them by choice and avoid the position that attract the mind to negative thought and be in the position that attract the mind to positive thought. For instance, if you sit and put your hand under your chin, you will attract negative thought to your mind but if you sit with your leg cross and look straight forward, you will attract positive thought to your mind, although looking straight forward with your eyes under your control in a comfortable position will attract positive thought to you.

HOLINESS

It is considered that holiness is a religious thing that pertain to a monk, a priest, a nun, and a highly religious person. Holiness is not a thing that pertain to a priest, a monk, a nun, nor a highly religious person alone. Holiness is a type of life that everybody should aspire to live.

As doing the right thing is what you allow yourself to do and what you do allow yourself to do, holiness is strictly what you do not allow yourself to do. Doing the right thing is a state of joyful worldly activities in an active life but holiness is a state of joyful worldly inactivity in a contented life.

Holiness is what you do not allow yourself to do in your everyday life. When you do not allow your mind to think any form of negative thought, when you do not allow yourself to talk any form of negative talk nor listen to a negative talk because listening to negative talk generate negative thought and when you do not allow yourself to act in a negative way and you strictly mind your business in thought, in words, and deed, you are a saint, you are a holy person whether you belong to a religion or not.

If you believe or think that it is not possible for you to become a holy person, the belief or the thought of the belief will make holiness to be impossible for you.

Holiness have so much to do with age, so also living the right life have much to do with experience which can also depend on age because the older you are the more experience you will have than the younger one in relation with life.

Doing the right thing lead to a righteous life. In practising righteousness, you may anger another person to set things right but in practicing holiness, you must not anger anyone, you must be solitary in mind even if you are among people. For instance, in the game of football that have a wide range of supporters, if you score a goal, you will anger the supporters of the other team and if you refuse to score a goal, you will anger the supporters of your team. To practice righteousness toward football which is doing the right thing, you must score a goal but to be holy, you are not to play football so that you will put yourself in the position that if you score a goal or not, you will not anger anyone.

Holiness is a state of worldly inactivity but because a young person is used to spending energy in worldly activities, if a young person try to become holy which is a state of inactivity in a joyful way, the young person will have excess energy and will become overfill with energy. If the excess energy is not directed by the young person, the energy will force the young person to any activity that is available which may be positive or negative and if it is negative, it will be similar to a dam river that will overflow and become destruction if it is not directed.

As one grow old, one will lose the ability to produce energy due to old age. As one lose the production of energy, one will not have excess energy that will need to be directed which make it easy for an old person to practice holiness which is a joyful state of worldly inactivity in a contended life.

If a young person aim to become holy, the young person must learn to direct his or her adrenalin through his or her thought because it is our thought that make our brain to direct the release of adrenalin to act. A young person that aspire to become holy must not dwell in idleness because idleness make the mind free to roam on different thought. Every young person must direct their energy to a course that will uplift the good in life so as to add to the development of life and should avoid anything that will disrupt life.

If anyone determine to live a holy life and strive everyday to become holy, with time the holiness that seem impossible and illusive will turn to a reality if one persist in becoming holy.

The misconception about holiness is that people think to become holy is to belong to a religion, dress in a particular way and pray or chant. Holiness is simply never to be angry at anyone and never to make anyone angry which can be difficult to practice without experience.

THE WORLD OF THOUGHT

There is a thought centre that connect every mind and it is the one that refuse to connect his or her mind to this thought centre negatively that can become holy. This mean that one should become solitary in thought and should only connect the mind to the thought that enhance the good in life. It is this thought centre that philosophy get it idea of universal mind for indeed it is a universal mind.

The universal mind is like a telephone control switchboard that interconnect every mind. This is why you will see that two people from a different place can have the same idea at the same time by connecting their mind to the universal mind to get inspiration from it because the universal mind have the record of everything in life.

The universal mind is neither good or evil, it is neutral to life. It is neither positive nor negative. The universal mind will reinforce you to be positive, if you are positive or will reinforce you to be negative if you are negative. It is the thought that you dwell upon that will add strength to the universal mind to reinforce you with it.

If you think within a frequency of thought, you will be connected to the frequency in the universal mind and influence you to more of its kind.

With the type of thought that you think, you will add strength to the frequency of the thought to influence other mind that think within the range of the frequency.

If you think a good thought, you are adding strength to the good in people and if you think an evil thought, you are adding strength to the evil in people. This is why punishment and reward are place on thought which make Jesus to command everyone to have a clean mind.

It is the type of thought that you accept into your mind that the universal mind will strengthen you with to either make you a good person or an evil person.

A thinking mind will make an idle mind to think, just as a swinging pendulum will make another pendulum to swing. If you think a type of thought the type of thought will make an idle mind to think in the same frequency and re-enforce other mind that think in that same frequency.

Because of the thought frequency, people that want to be holy prefer to live in a monastery or in a secluded place.

If one live in a monastery or in seclusion, it will be easy for one to become holy but only in seclusion. If something takes one out of the seclusion, one will not be able to withstand the pressure outside the seclusion because there is no pressure in seclusion that work against holiness.

For you to strong in holiness and be able to withstand the pressure of the negative force in the society, you don't need to live in a secluded place. What you have to do is to build the inner strength through the experience of meeting the world to withstand the negative force that will come to you through your environment.

By living in the world, you are to close yourself to the negative vibration of the world.

You may be far from another person but if your mind is of the same vibration with the person's mind, your mind and the person's mind will become connected and influence each other.

For you to be holy, you must make your mind strong that no other mind should be able to influence your mind to evil. It should be your mind that should be influencing other mind to live a good life. Make your mind strong that it should be attracting other mind to the frequency of the vibration of your thought because the strong always attract the weak. You can achieve this by becoming calm and personal and strongly direct your mind to your aim without doubt. Do not fantasize over your aim because fantasy lead to mental weakness. You should not think back and forth nor should you allow your mind to become confuse for a confused mind is a weak mind and will be attracted by other mind to their frequency of vibration.

If you can become clam, you will become close to every frequency of thought like a switch off phone that is close to other phone and when you think, you will become open to the frequency of the vibration of the type of thought you are thinking.

THE CONTROL OF THE MIND

The mind is the hardest thing to control but with persistence practice, one can control his or her mind.

The control of the mind depend on the determination to control it but one will always forget to control the mind because one is not use to the act of the control of the mind. One will always forget to control the mind because it has not become a habit but no one should be discouraged to control his or her mind even if it seem hard to control. Anytime you forget to control your mind, start to control it immediately you remember.

Many people think that it is easy to tame a wild horse than to tame the mind but this type of thought concerning the mind make the mind to be difficult to control. If one think that it is difficult to control the mind, it will be difficult for the person to control his or her mind but if one think it is easy to control the mind, it will be less difficult for the person to control his or her mind.

The first point to start from in controlling the mind is to be able to calm the mind without the use of drug or stimulant.

The mind is of the nature that it wants to respond to anything that passes through it. When any thought pass through your mind, do not respond to it. If you are for or against anything that pass through your mind, you will not be calm, you will become agitated but when you let everything that pass through your mind alone, your mind will be calm.

To control your mind, you must not be angry at anyone and you must not make anyone angry. Anger is an emotional state that easily take control of the mind negatively.

If you are angry at anyone, you will not be able to direct your mind positively and it you make anyone angry, the anger that the person will direct at you will attract your mind to the frequency of anger if you did not have the inner strength to remain calm.

To control your mind, you must not let desire to take root in your mind in any form. To desire is a sign that you are alive but you should learn to be content, do not let your desire to control you.

If you have money, you can buy anything good things that your heart desire but if you don't have money, do not desire what you cannot afford because if you desire what you cannot afford, it may lead you to temptation and your mind will become chaotic which may manifest as confusion in your life.

You should not respond to the desire of the body. When the desires of the body arise, leave the desire alone if you cannot satisfy it at the moment. Do not add thought to it nor should you try to remove the thought of the desire from your mind. If you do any of this, you will be enforcing the desire with the energy for your mind to resist your control. If you leave the desire of the body the way it is, within a short time, the desire will fade away by itself except if someone is hypnotizing you.

To control your mind, you must not defend yourself verbally in a negative way nor should you struggle with anyone because they will have effect on your mind to resist control.

Defending yourself verbally in a negative way will create disturbance for you and enhance the one you are defending yourself against to more fight. If a person hit you and you did not respond, the person may hit you again so that you can respond and if you did not respond, the person may hit you hard so that you can respond and if you have the inner strength to remain calm, the person attacking you will feel defeated because you are a peaceful person and the person is not peaceful. If you did not respond to an angry person, you are superior to the angry person but if you respond to an angry person, you are of the same kind with the angry person.

Calmness of the mind is the key to the control of the mind. If you are able to calm your mind, you will be able to control what you think and what you should not think.

To calm the mind is the key to holiness. In the old world, Hindu mystic live in seclusion, so that they will not meet what that will agitate their mind that will make them not to be holy and in this new world, religious mystic live in monastery for the same reason. Living in seclusion can make one to be holy but because one is not expose to the pressure of the world will make one to be inexperience in certain issue that one have to be diplomatic with.

Holiness and living the right life is the key to life and the gateway to the perfect city of God. Jesus said that many will enter the kingdom of God from the east to the west which mean that any person that is holy and living the right life, whether the person is a Hindu, a Muslim or whatever the person is will enter the kingdom of God. It is the one that can become holy and know how to do the right thing that will gain entry to the perfect city where everything is perfection.

Everything you will become depend on your health and your health depend on your fate and your fate depend on the way you are living your life.
If you are not in good health, you cannot have the strength to do the right thing and as you did not have the strength to do the right thing, you will also not have the strength to do the wrong thing but you will still need to control your mind.

To refuse to act may seem to take energy because holiness is the refusal to act in a certain way. For example, to refuse to have sex when you and an extreme beautiful opposite sex are naked in a close room or to keep calm and silent when someone is verbally attacking you will take energy. Adrenalin will give you surplus energy to react but you can control the adrenalin and use it as the energy to stop yourself from reacting.

To live a calm life, you must not fight against evil nor should you live the life of fighting against evil which is a life of good and evil, a life of duality. Know that evil will always destroy itself at it own time because this is an adamant law of life.

If you fight against evil, evil will be there for you to fight against and if you continue to fight against evil, evil will continue to be there for you to fight against. Fighting evil will also make you be evil because fight itself is evil.

There is no need to fight against evil. If you don't want evil, become good, even to the point of pain to yourself and with time, evil will cease to exist for you and you will become like the Midas touch that turn everything he touch to gold.

Jesus Christ have the great power to fight against evil but he refuse to fight evil and he endure evil to the point of death and with his death, he change the history of the world. Jesus said that we should not resist an evil person – Matthew chapter 5 verses 39. If you resist evil, you are giving the evil strength to persist it and resistance cause friction.

In every evil that you resist, something positive will be subtracted from you and in every evil that you did not resist, something positive will be added to you.

Do not see evil in anyone because if you refuse to see evil in anyone, there will be no evil for you to resist, although it take great inner calmness for you not to see evil in anyone.

If you are living a holy life and doing the right thing, anything that an evil person take from you will be given back to you in a multiple fold, like the case of Job that went through severe pain and hardship without cursing God nor complain against men, and what was taken from him was given to him in a multiple fold and his end was far better than his beginning.

Everyone have within his or her mind a nature that is prone to negativity, an aspect of the mind that is weak to succumb to the temptation of evil. Anyone that want to eradicate evil from his or her mind must make the weak aspect of the mind that is prone to succumb to the temptation of evil to become strong and resist negativity.

Repentance, which is the eradication of the negative aspect of the mind that is prone to evil is not as easy as many people think it is. To lay aside worldly indulgence, the love of ease, and the gratification of the senses is not as easy as many people think it is and after some struggle, many people give up in despair.

To live a positive life is not one minute struggle and it is not a day struggle. It is a struggle that everyone have to contend with all through his or her life time till he or she depart this life and it is only those that endure to the end that will win.

Undivided attention in your everyday life which is concentrating your mind in whatever you are doing at the moment, leaving the past behind and focusing on the step that will lead to the future is what that will make everyone pass through this struggle successfully.

Whatever you focus your attention on will displace any other thought in your mind. Use this process to overcome the temptation to negativity by the focus of your attention on what you want which will displace the negative nature of the mind.

If you think, think attentively so that negative thought will not come to your mind through what you think and thereby close the avenue to negativity.

If you do anything wrong by mistake, do not hold the wrong against yourself and do not hold any wrong against anyone. To hold wrong against yourself or against anyone will attract negativity to your mind and if you allow this to your mind, negativity will start growing in your mind till you become negative. When you do anything wrong by mistake, correct yourself and go on with life without thinking of it because you must let the past be the past for there is nothing that exist except what that is in the present.

Many people cannot change themselves but they will like the other person to change and they will want to change the other person. The reality is that it is difficult to change oneself and since it is difficult to change oneself, it is much more difficult to change another person.

If you want the other person to change, you have to change yourself first and set yourself as an example for the other person to change. You cannot change another person with force because you will appear a terror to the person and you cannot change another person with begging because you will appear a weakling to the person. The gate of change is in the mind of the individual which can only be open by the individual through conviction when his or her experience tally with a good teaching that will open the gate of change in the person.

THE LAW THAT GOVERN LIFE

5

My son, do not forget my law, let your heart keep my commandment, for length of days and long life and peace they will add to you – King Solomon

THE LAW AND LIFE

Everything in life is govern by law from the sun which is very large to the atom which is very small. The law govern what that can be seen and what that cannot be seen with the eyes. The law govern the physical and the spiritual for the law itself is life.

The law that govern life are in two perspective. The first perspective is the law that govern the chemistry of life and the mechanism of life and the second perspective is the law that govern emotion which govern how the animated act and react.

To know the law that govern the chemistry of life and the mechanism of life is to study the science of nature which have a wide coverage which is not the aim of this book for there are many books in the subject of the science of nature. The aim of this book is to understand the law that govern human emotion because it is our emotion that govern our life.

There are many books that teach the subject of how you can get what you want but they will not work for you if you neglect to live by the law that govern your emotion which the keeping of them depend on the control of your mind.

Everything that happen to you or that will happen to you depend on your fate and your fate depend on the law that you keep and the law that you did not keep which both depend on your emotion.

If you obey the law that govern life, you obey it for your own good but to obey the law that govern life depend on how you control your emotion. If you disobey the law that govern life, you disobey it for your own evil but to disobey the law that govern life depend on the letting lose of your emotion.

If you keep keeping the law of life, the law of life will keep keeping you in the direction that you keep it and if you keep breaking the law of life, the law of life will keep breaking you in the direction that you break it.

If you are not going forward in any area of your life, it mean that you are living against the law that govern that area of your life.

It is hard to keep all the law of life because it is hard to completely control your emotion and it is easy to live against the law that govern life because it is easy for your emotion to control you.

Learn to master your emotion and let your emotion be your servant instead of it to be your master.

The Law That Govern Honor

The most important to honor is God. To honor God is to honor the law that govern life and strictly live by it. We are to honor God with all our life but to honor God is to honor our neighbor and to honor our neighbor is to attract honor to ourself. Everyone like to be honored which make it important to honor everyone whether young or old.

You are to honor your father and mother in a special way because they are responsible for your life up to the point that you can take care of yourself. Some people may say that if not for their parent they will not have come to this sinful world that is full of negativity and because of this, they will not give their parent a special honor that is due to them. Some may also say that their parent are responsible for their bad condition because their parent was not able to give them good education or a good start in life, may be due to the financial state of their parent or due to ignorant of the parent and because of this they will not like to give their parent the due special honor that their parent deserve.

Whatever condition that anyone is in or what type of parent that give birth to one is the result of the person's fate which is the result of a past life. It is the fate that you create for yourself that lead you to the type of parent that will make you pay for the wrong you did to life. God is not a partial God that will make one child to go to a good parent and another child to go to a bad parent. Every child will go to the type of parent that they deserve. One coming to this earth life is an opportunity that nature give us through our parent to pay our moral and spiritual debt that we owe life. The role of our parent is to give us the ground to excel and take care of us up to the stage that we can take care of ourselves and for this role, they deserve a special honor whether they fulfill it or not.

To honor your parent did not mean that you will always be around them if you are independent of them. To honor your parent mean that you will not do anything that is against their wish if the wish is not hostile to you or hostile to life.

You are to honor the aged with a special honor for they deserve a special honor because of their old age. To honor the aged is to show consideration and respect for them in every condition.

You must honor those in authority with a special honor because they run the affairs of the state. You must honor them whether they run the affairs of your state in a right way or not because without them, the state will be chaotic. Some people don't vote because they think that the government is bad but without a government, everyone cannot have a peaceful sleep when there is no government to run the affairs of the state.

The honor that you are to give to those in authority is to obey every law that they make concerning the affairs of the state. If you think that a law is wrong, you can petition the government for amendment.

You are to honor your teacher with a special honor because they teach you and without a teacher, you will not be knowledgeable. To honor your teacher is to obey their rule concerning teaching you.

Most of all, the way you live your life will attract honor or dishonor to you and for this reason, you should live a good life that will attract honor to you.

Use silent to create honor for yourself for the more you speak, the common you will appears and the more likely you may say something that is wrong or someone may misunderstand you.

The Law That Govern Killing

Some religion are strictly against killing that they will never kill any animated living thing because they believe that as you and I have the right to life, so every animated living thing have the right to life.

Life is in strata and the upper strata feed on the lower strata to stay alive. Plant that have life but is not animated feed on minerals that have no life. Animals that have life and are animated feed on plant that have life but are not animated. In the animal world, the more intelligent or the more powerful feed on the less intelligent or the less powerful and human that is most intelligent feed on them all, both the animated and the inanimated.

The killing of a lower animal by a higher animal is base on reason which is to feed and stay alive and this is the only reason permitted by nature to kill. Nature only permit killing so as to stay alive and any other reason for killing beside this is against the law that govern life.

You must not kill anyone for any reason, not even if the person kill another person for this is the responsibility of the government of your state.

The Law That Govern Giving

It is the unconscious fear of poverty that make many people to unconsciously fear to give probably base on the poverty of their past or base on their present state of insecurity. What many people fail to realize is that a giver cannot lack and a person that lack cannot give. If you have and you refuse to give when someone beg from you, by the law of attraction, a form of lack will be attracted to you and the lack may come in the form of what you wanted most in life.

In the angle of lending, if you lend money to anyone in affliction, you must not impose interest on the money because if you impose interest on the money, you are showing lack in your own life and the blessing that accrue to giving will not come to you.

If you lend to the afflicted and you impose interest, you are adding to the person's affliction and nature will take away the interest from you in another form.

If anyone come to beg from you, you should give it, if you have it within your reach. You should not tell the person to wait till tomorrow, not even the next moment when you are not busy.
Sometime giving to a lazy person can enhance the laziness but you should not look at this in giving. If a person choose to be lazy, the person is lazy for himself or herself but laziness is due to when the body lack iron that supply oxygen to the brain and other part of the body and also when the body lack some of the B vitamin that aid to extract energy from the food that we eat.

In giving help, you must not be selective and you should not consider any help before you give the needed help.
If you see somebody that you consider to be an enemy or consider you to be an enemy need help in an unconscious state, you must give the needed help without fail and you must not consider anyone to be an enemy because we are all part of the whole for there is nobody that is the whole itself.
Anything that you give to life whether good or bad will surely come back to you, in every action there are equal and opposite reaction.
If you refuse to give help to anyone that is in an unconscious state, you will also need help in an unconscious state and it will not be given to you. It take great inner strength to help anyone that is against you but the reward that you will get for helping someone that is against you will be greater than the reward that you will get for helping someone that is for you.

If your brother or sister become poor or is financially weak and come to you for sustenance, you must help him or her with the needed help without fail. You must not take interest in whatever you give to him or her whatever the condition may be and you must not impose any condition on the money. You must give your brother or sister the needed help as much as he or she need without any form of complain, you must generously open your hand to him or her.

The Law That Govern Anger

Anger is an emotional state that is highly destructive and when anyone allow anger to dwell in his or her mind is always beyond the control of the person.

The emotion of anger is negative, no matter what one direct the anger to. Anger is destructive to the cell of the body which make the body to age more than it chronological years. Nothing is durable in the life of an extremely angry person and anger bring obstacle to the path of the one that indulge in it.

Anger is arouse due to the vain ego that we possess which make us unable to tolerate many things. Anger is also arouse due to the inability to endure negative people.

Anger have chain reaction that make one to react to other situation long after the cause of the anger have gone and it is due to holding the thought of the cause of the anger in the mind.

The thought of the cause of anger always want one to take vengeance and vengeance is against the law that govern life. For we to avoid vengeance, we must not think of the negative things that another person did to us. When more than two angry people have anger in the same direction come together, they form a crowd of angry people directing anger to a particular purpose and it is extremely destructive.

The secret behind religion is when more than two people come together to direct their mind to a purpose, the purpose always take form and become effective which make every religion whether good or bad to be real. For this reason, you must avoid where angry people come together so that you will not unconsciously add strength to their anger with your thought.

The person that is fill with anger always respond to negative situations angrily and thereby stir contention and your response to an angry person will either calm the anger or elevate the anger.

To some people, anger is a health problem similar to the case of insanity when disease damage a certain neuron in the brain, the person will always respond angrily to any situation that is not favorable to the person.

For you not to breed anger and discord, you should overlook transgression and thereby breed peace. For you to aid peace, you must overlook many things for your inability to adjust yourself to many people will attract anger which will disrupt peace.

If you note a sign of anger in a place, leave the place immediately even if the anger did not concern you because it is what you see that your mind will register and if your mind register anger, by the law of attraction, angry situation will be attracted to you. This is the meaning of the saying that we should not walk on land that angel fear to thread.

Do not argue in a negative way over anything because argument lead to unconscious anger that may surface if the argument persist. If you notice a sign of argument in your discussion, stop the discussion at once. You must avoid argument with all your strength and do not say anything that will lead to argument.

It is anger that result to quarrel because when one lose the control of his or her mind to anger, quarrel may be the result but quarrel bring difficult situation to one's life, a wise person must avoid it.

Anyone that permit himself or herself to lose control to anger is stupidity on the part of the one. We must live our life to be above all annoyance and learn to tolerate the individual negativity.

It is anger that make anyone want to pay evil for evil and if you pay evil for evil, it will make you to be evil.

Do not pay evil for evil, obey the law of life and trust that life will give to you what you give to it, therefore do not indulge in evil in thought and deed.

Many things that people are angry over are base on assumption. Anger cloud reason which lead to more assumption. To act base on assumption is foolishness because many things are not the way they seem to be.

Remove anyone that bring anger in others from your company so that contention may not be in your company. If you realize that anyone in your company is so negative that the person always bring out anger in people, you must remove the person from your circle if you have the power to do so and if you did not have the power to do so, stay away from the circle of the person.

Stay away from a person that is given to anger and be far from the one that is bad tempered that you may not become familiar with his or her ways to lay a snare for yourself. Characters are contagious, avoid people with the character that you do not want.

The Law That Govern Desire

It is the want within the mind called desire that lead to various form of temptation.

When you allow desire to be planted in your mind, the desire will start growing in your mind till it cloud every good reason pertaining what you desire if you desire it negatively or if what you desire is negative which will lead you to carry the desire out against every good reason.

Desire come to us through what we see and hear and for this reason, you must be strict with what you allow yourself to see and hear.

The way to destroy desire is never to give it attention whenever it arise in your mind, neither rejecting nor accepting it because if you do, you are giving it attention, and you are giving it energy to wrestle with you.

Strengthen your mind with calmness so that any form of thought that lead to desire will not find entrance to your mind.

When you desire anything that belong to another, judgement will be place on you even if you did not carry out the desire because everything you do start from thought which extend to deed.

The Law That Govern Rest

In the law of thermodynamic, it is stated that energy cannot be created or destroyed but are transform from one form to another.

Energy is transferred from the food we eat to our body and energy is transferred from our body to the work we do. In doing work, the energy that is being transferred will become depleted within a period of time, so everybody need to rest so as to recover the depleted energy.

According to the law, six days is meant for work and the seventh day is meant for rest, although according to the modern calendar, there are five working days in a week.

If you find rest difficult because you see rest as a waste of time, other people that are working with you must rest on the seventh day of work if they want to.

You should schedule your daily work for your workers to rest between the working hours so as to develop more strength to work and be able to work attentively and be of a sane mind.

The Law That Govern Sex

The issue of sex is a critical issue because people that cannot control their sex life think that we should give free reign to sex. Some think that if we desire sex, we should not resist the desire.

Because sex have mental sweetness and the thought of it bring pleasure to some people make them think that we should not deny ourselves of this sweetness but every sweet have it bitter because we are living in a dual world where everything is duality.

Some people can be so debase that they can have sex with their parent. It is a strict law that no one should have sex with his or her father or mother if the person don't want to see the extreme bitterness of sex. You must not see the nakedness of your parent. It is a taboo.

I hear of a town that their male will have sex with their mother before marriage and they say that the mother is teaching her son how to have sex with a woman. I don't think this practice still exist because modern religion have change many things in an uncivilized society. This act originate from a negative god called the god of sex.

You must not have sex with your father's wife, it is the nakedness of your father and you must not see her nakedness.

It is a double crime to have sex with your father's wife because a crime of adultery is added to it even thought she is your father's wife.

You must not have sex with your sister or brother, the daughter or the son of your father or mother whether born in the same household or born outside it.

You must not have sex with the daughter of your son or the daughter of your daughter, you must not see their nakedness because they are your nakedness.

You must not have sex with the daughter of your father's wife, she is your sister, you must not see her nakedness.

You must not have sex with your father's sister, she is the blood relation of your father. You must not have sex with your mother's sister, she is the blood relation of your mother.

You must not have sex with your father's brother, you must not have sex with his wife, she is your aunt.

You must not have sex with your daughter inlaw, you must not see have nakedness, she is your son's wife.

You must not have sex with your brother's wife, you must not see her nakedness, it is the nakedness of your brother.
In some culture in Africa, they do have sex with their brother's wife when their brother is far away in a distant land for a long time. This culture is still in existence and it is a negative culture that everyone should run away from.

You must not have sex with a woman and her daughter. The daughter of her son and the daughter of her daughter you must not have sex with, they are cases of blood relation.

You must not take a woman in addition to her sister as a rival to have sex with, that is beside her during her lifetime.

You must not lie down with a male the same as you lie with a woman.

You must not have sex with another man's wife.

In some culture in Africa, when their best friend visit them, they entertain this best friend with their wife to have sex with when the best friend spend the night with the friend. This is similar to group sex in America and Europe.

These are the law that govern sex for those that give free reign to sex but to those that want to live a meaningful life toward sex, sex is the union of two soul therefore one should only have sex with the person they are to share their life with.

Some people support masturbation as an act of releasing sexual passion but masturbation is an extreme waste of sexual energy.

The Law That Govern Stealing

People steal for various reasons. Some steal to satisfy their need, some steal to satisfy their want, while some steal to satisfy their greed. Every reason behind stealing have different punishment attach to the stealing.

The person that steal to satisfy his or her need will be punish by nature less than the person that steal to satisfy his or her want and the person that steal to satisfy his or her greed will be severely punish by nature.

No one should steal for any reason because the least punishment for stealing is to pay between two times to seven times of what was stolen when in need depending on the state of the theft because the person is in need.

The Law That Govern Justice

Every country have their code of justice and the code of justice of every country are not so different from each other.

Every religion have their code of justice which are nearly the same except some which are bizarre.

Injustice in judgement is against the law of life and no one should show favor to a friend in judgement and no one should show favor to the rich in judgement over the poor.

It is fear that make people to favor the rich in judgement and it is this same fear that will destroy the one that favor the rich in judgement. It is injustice to prefer the person of great one than the person of lesser one.

You must not commit injustice in measurement which is deception. Measurement are reduce by some people due to greed propel by the desire for riches which always lead to poverty.

The Law That Govern Thought

Our thought are spiritual energy that shape itself to reality, not according to our intention but according to what we think. It is our mind that shape our life due to the type of thought that we allow to dwell in it therefore we should guard our mind against any form of negative thought for our life spring from what we think.

Everything that we do start from our thought and if we allow every thought to enter our mind, the thought will attract similar thought to our mind and influence us to act according to the thought. You may not be aware of it but with the passing of time, you will see that you are acting according to the thought that dwell in your mind.

Your thought have energy of their own and work by itself. If you persistently think a thought, within a period of time, the thought will take form and shape itself to reality.

If two people are thinking opposite thought, it is the one with the strongest energy which is the one that is given full attention to that will take effect.

It is the strong that displace the weak, any thought that is stronger than the thought in your mind will displace the thought in your mind and take the control of your mind to manifest in your life. This is the secret of spiritual attack.

Train your mind to be calm and make it strong in calmness so that any other thought will not find entrance to your mind.

A calm mind boost the immune system and see things the way they are because a calm mind don't assume things but a troubled mind depress the immune system and exaggerate things.

When the mind is calm, the brain release endorphin, a substance that make one feel good and elated and endorphin is a natural pain killer.

Hard drug like cocaine, heroine, and opium mimic endorphin by binding to the endorphin receptor thereby creating the feeling of elation artificially in the brain. The hard drug prevent the mind from it natural calmness by blocking the endorphin receptor which make all hard drug to create withdrawal symptom. Withdrawal symptom is the inability to stop using a drug. The more one take hard drug, the more it will be difficult for one to stop taking the hard drug because they will become restless without taking the hard drug. When they continue to take the hard drug, it will get to a point that the hard drug will collapse their body system which may lead to death if there is no immediate medical attention.

Calmness of mind lead to long life but distortion in it age the body cell which lead to aging of the body which make one older than his or her age.

If your mind is calm, you will not become discourage in the day of distress. You will have mental strength which will lead to courage in the day of distress but if you are living negatively, your mind will be weak and you will become discourage on the day that fate will be against you.

Anyone that can rule his or her mind will be greater than a ruler of a city for it is easy to rule a city than to rule the mind. It take mental strength to control the mind which depend on the way you are living your life and if anyone cannot control his or her mind, the person will be similar to a dustbin that accept everything that is drop into it.

It is living against the law that govern life that debase the mind and for anyone to live a noble life, such one must live in accord with the law that govern life.

The Law That Govern Words

We think in picture but because we cannot express our thought in picture which is telepathy, we learn to speak so that we can express our thought in words. Telepathy sometime happen between two people when one realize that he or she is feeling the thought of the other person.

The words that we speak have effect not according to our thought but according to the meaning of the words which another person interpret to himself or herself.

When you speak many words, some of these words may not be according to what you intend to speak especially when you are in the state of anger which make it good for everyone not to speak when there is the tendency to be anger.

When you speak too much or when you allow your mouth to be faster than your mind, you will speak what you did not intend to speak and the more you speak, the more you will be liable to speak something wrong.

We consider what we speak to be trivial but death and life are in the power of what we speak which is govern by what we think which lead to what we do. Every words that we speak is the reflection of what we think which is what we store in our mind whether consciously or unconsciously.

Think before you answer because your yes suppose to mean yes and your no suppose to mean no. When you say yes and you mean no will lead you to a debase life and will make many people to look down on you. If you are not sure of what to say, ask to be given time so that you can think over it and answer in a proper way.

You must be careful of the words that you let out of your mouth because you will become negative through any unprofitable words that you speak. As you must not speak unprofitable words you must not listen to unprofitable words so as not to pollute your consciousness and thereby open yourself to negative frequency that will attract negative thought to you.

Do not let immoral word out of your mouth. Let only words that are beneficial for good hearing and for building up that will impart what is favorable to the hearer only come out of your mouth.

Do not let bitterness to be in you and bitterness always lead to negative words.

Everyone respond differently to negative situation which depend on the individual understanding and the level of individual tolerance and endurance. Learn to respond positive to negative situation.

You must avoid debate because debate lead to mental tension and hostile feeling when it is negative.

You should not look down on anyone but be an example to everyone in speaking and in living a moral life. Anything you do will influence someone to do the same thing.

You must not speak injurious of anyone and do not condemn anyone. Put yourself in the position of others and be reasonable and mild to all.

Be a good listener and be slow to speak. Shun foolish questioning and argument over the law, they are unprofitable and futile.

In speaking with another person, you should listen attentively so as to understand the reason behind what the person is saying so that you can give a reasonable answer to the understanding of the person.

The Law That Govern Integrity

To live in integrity is the quality of being honest and having a strong moral principle.

Integrity is the quality that will make one a positive person but it is this quality that many people neglect.

If your associate is doing something that will downrate his or her integrity, you must disassociate yourself from the person because character are contagious. If you did not disassociate yourself from a person that is downrating his or her integrity, you will start to be in agreement with the person's character which will reflect in your character.

If you downrate your integrity and you start to live a foolish life, your ways will be right in your own eyes but if you develop the sense to listen to counsel and take correction, you will upgrade your integrity.

If you associate with the wise, you will become wise but if you associate with the foolish, you will become foolish because the character of your associate will reflect in you.

The wise build his or her life by walking with the wise but the foolish tear his or her life down by walking with the foolish. For you to be wise and remain wise, you must choose the type of people you associate with carefully.

The person that is neglecting discipline will not have integrity and will come to poverty but the one taking correction will be leaded to integrity and a good life.

There are different types of poverty. There is poverty of the mind, there is poverty of health and there is poverty of money. When you neglect discipline, discipline will discipline you with one of these poverty and when you take to correction, many ill will be corrected in your life.

The ways of a man or woman are pure in his or her own eyes but life always make estimate of what every person do.

Many people always think that they are justified in their act. A thief will tell you the reason for his or her theft, a liar will tell you the reason for his or her lies, and a prostitute will tell you the reason for prostitution and they are all base on self deception. It may not be bad if someone deceive you but it is bad if you deceive yourself.

A person with integrity is the person that keep the law that govern life and by keeping the law that govern life, one is keeping his or her life out of trouble.

The person that despise integrity is the person that despise the law that govern life which will lead the person to self destructive life and death.

Happy are the children of the one that live in integrity for the way you live your life will reflect in the life of your children which is the spiritual effect of your life on your children. When you live the life of integrity, it will lead you to riches, honor and glory which your children may inherit from you.

The Law That Govern Love

Love is what everybody whether consciously or unconsciously wanted most in their life, yet love is what many people did not understand. What many people call love is self centred conditional love.

God is love and this love extend to us. We are created in the image and likeness of the love of God. If we are to love which is of God that we were created in it likeness, we are to love without attaching condition to it. If we love and attach condition to it, we are self centred because we consider our interest without the consideration of the interest of the one we claim to love.

To love is to consider the interest of the person you love and also consider your own interest or you consider the interest of the person you love with your own interest side by side.

If you lack love or the people that you love don't love you, it mean that you are expressing anger when you are suppose to express love because life will give to us what we give to it.

There are two types of love which are general love and personal love. General love is the love that you are to give to everyone, be it a friend or a foe while personal love is the love that you are to give to those that are close to you.

Many people give personal love in the place of general love to those that are not close to them which sometime lead to a negative end. If someone that is not close to you need something that you have and you give the person without the person asking the thing from you, you are displaying personal love in the place of general love which mean that you are interfering in what that did not concern you. But if the person beg the thing from you, whether the person is a friend or foe, you are to give it.

You can display personal love to a group of people, a community, or a nation because in this case, it is the one that wanted it that will take part in the share of the love but you must not display it to an individual that did not concern you. You are a part of a people, you are part of a community, and you are part of a nation which make it for you to display personal love to a people, a community and a nation without they begging from you but an individual that did not concern you are not part of you, therefore if you display personal love to them, you are breaking the law of interference.

There are some individual that need your help but they do not have the opportunity to ask you, you can help these people without begging from you because if they have the opportunity to beg from you, they will beg from you. There are some individual that have the opportunity to beg from you but will not want to beg from you, you must not help these individual until they beg from you because their refusal to beg from you mean that they did not want help and you should only help them if they want your help by begging from you.

If somebody that is against you fall, you must not rejoice because if you rejoice, it will have effect on your love life and it will make you the same with the person because you are now against the person.

If you lack love in your life, you should give love under every condition to everyone. You should give to anyone that beg from you because anything that you give will come back to you through what you lack in your life.

The thought of hate attract hate. If you give hate, hate will come to you through the one that is close to you and if you give love, love will come to you through the one that is close to you.

Love don't go to the one that want it, love go to the one that give it and because of this, you should give love under every condition.

Do not have anything against anyone and do not do anything negative that will make anyone to have something against you. You should adjust your life to the life of everyone.

Do not resist anyone that is negative in a negative way because if you do, you will become negative. A negative person will be attracted to you only if there is a form of negativity in you which will serve as the point of attraction for the negative person to be attracted to you. If you are positive, you will repel a negative person and if you are negative, you will repel a positive person.

Love your enemy and do not curse the one that persecute you. The love that you are suppose to show to your enemy is a general love and not a personal love because many people did not understand the statement "love your enemy". The curse that many people curse their enemy is due to ignorant because the reality of life is that anything you do to another person whether a friend or an enemy, you do to yourself, so if you curse your enemy, you are cursing yourself. If any person is persecuting you, do not have hostile feeling within your mind against the person because if you do, you will become a negative person.

When you gossip or judge another person, it did not show love in you, it show that a form of negativity is dwelling in you, when you judge or gossip another person, someone will judge and gossip you. In every word that you speak, you must not speak any word that will downgrade another person.

For you to live a life of love, you must avoid negative people and you must avoid those that keep company with the bad tempered, the drinker, the covetous, the gossip, the non-stop talker, the greedy, the reviler, and the hard to get along with so that they don't stand as a point of attraction of these people to you.

The type of character of people you mix with will reflect in your character and you will not reflect the character of the people you avoid. The company that you keep will become part of you.

You should not become a stumbling block to another person because whatever negative thing you do can make another person stumble.

If you do something that is negative, the negativity will influence another person to be negative if the person is in agreement with the negativity. What people see influence their character in a positive or negative way depending on the angle that the person view life from and the person's level of insecurity. Therefore, every thought that you think, every word that you speak and everything that you do will influence another person to be either a positive person or a negative person and the effect will fall back on you.

Do not be a sharer in the evil of others, preserve yourself chaste. When you support the negative act of another person either in thought, words, or deed, you will have share in their evil. Because of this, do not waste time, energy or peace of mind on what that did not concern you, strictly mind your business.

The Law That Govern Lust

Lust is something that attract our mind that we give in to. If you become lust to the beauty of the senses, it will attract temptation to you and if your strength is weak to resist the temptation, you will succumb to the temptation.

Temptation show you where you are weak and any temptation that you succumb to show that you are extremely weak to the cause of the temptation. The more you succumb to temptation, the weaker you will become to resist temptation.

The more you resist temptation, the more you will overcome temptation and the more strength you will develop to overcome temptation.

When you think of material things, you will open your mind to the temptation of materialism. When you speak of material things or when you speak of your success or failure, you will open the mind of those hearing you to the temptation of materialism. For you not to open your mind to the temptation of materialism, do not think of them but your thought are govern by what you see and hear and the way you interpret what you see and hear to yourself combine with your level of insecurity. For you not to open the mind of people to material things do not speak of your success or failure to the one that it did not concern.

You should not be anxious over anything because what you justly earn will come to you. It is your past that will determine your present because you cannot sow rice in your past and reap beans in your present and it is your present that will determine your future.

If you are living the right life and you continue to live the right life, what you justly earn will come to you and you will not need to search for things that bring happiness for they will follow as a consequence. If you are living a wrong life and you continue to live the wrong life, things that you want will be diverted from you and your life will be one step forward and two step backward. If you strictly live in accord with the law that govern life, you will not need to search for things that bring gladness, they will certainly follow you as the result of the good life you are living.

You must work to earn what you want so that you will not lack and create room for lust in any area of your life. You must provide for every member of your family so as not to create room for lust to any of them.

You should be content with what you have except if you have the potential for more. We brought nothing to this world and we will leave with nothing except the various fate that we create to ourselves. To be content did not mean that you will not strive to live a better life, to be content mean that you should not desire anything out of lust.

STRENGTH AND WEAKNESS

It is mental weakness that make anyone to live against the law that governs life that makes one to become negative. The more negative you are, the more you will become because the more you are negative, the more you will attract negativity to yourself.

If you can summon the inner strength to become positive, the more positive that you are, the more positive you will become and the more you will attract the positive to yourself.

Any law that you break will stand against your progress in an area of your life for a period of time and until this period expire, no form of progress will come to you in that area of your life.

When you allow your mind to become negative by anger, fear, jealousy, sorrow, regret, and procrastination, it will be difficult for you to be positive and when you let your mind to become calm, focus, and confident, it will be easy for you to be positive.

Unnecessary talk, joke, and negative desire make the mind weak and any form of weakness will make you not to have strength to keep the law that govern life.

The law did not care if you are an atheist, a monotheist, or a polytheist. If you keep keeping the law, the law will keep rewarding you and if you keep breaking the law, the law will keep punishing you.

The law did not care if you are rich or poor. The law did not care if you are in good health or in bad health. The law did not care if you are living or dying. The law did not care whether you keep it yesterday and break it today. If you keep keeping the law, the law will keep keeping you in the proportion that you keep it and if you keep breaking the law, the will keep breaking you in the proportion that you break it.

Ignorant is not an excuse for breaking the law but you cannot keep a law that you did not know although everyone have conscience that will tell what is good and what is bad but our conscience depend on the level of our understanding.

When you don't know a law and you break the law, life will punish you less than the one that know the law and break it. When you know a law and you understand the law and you break it, life will severely punish you especially if you are a teacher of the law e.g a priest that understand the law and an inspirational speaker that understand the law. A scientist that know and understand the law will be severely punished by the law for breaking it whether the scientist is religious or not.

THE

SECRET

OF

SPIRITUAL

POWER

6

He that is ruling his spirit is greater than he that is ruling a city – King Solomon

THE POWER OF LIFE

There is only one power that stream through life and animate everything in life and this power is life itself. The power is the law that govern life and it is life itself.

The power of life that stream through we human is in our mind which animate us through our thought. This power is the you which animate you and make you to be you which lie in your directed thought that make up the you that you are.

The power that animate life is neutral to life and this power manifest in our mind through our thought.

Our mind is neither good nor evil, it is the purpose that we direct it that make it good or evil. It is similar to fire that is neither good nor evil but the purpose that we direct it to that make fire to be a good thing or an evil thing. When you use fire to create, you are using fire for a good purpose but when you use fire to destroy, you are using fire for an evil purpose for fire itself is neutral to life.

As fire is neutral to life, so our mind is neutral to life and what we direct our mind to govern our life which make us to be a good person or an evil person.

The power that stream through life which manifest as our thought will obey our command if we persistently direct it to what we want to be and will manifest to reality. If you direct your mind to a thought to a good purpose and it manifest to reality, the good will return to bless you and if you direct your mind to a thought to an evil purpose and it manifest to reality, the evil will return to curse you.

Some people use external power, like the power of the black art, sorcery, and black magic to do their will. Black art, sorcery, and black magic don't work for everybody. They work only for the people that are in the same vibration with the black art, sorcery, and black magic, people that have the same element of evil with them. This is why the black art, sorcery, and black magic don't work on advance people, people that are advance in knowledge of life which is knowledge of light, which make advance people not to believe in them. The black art, sorcery, and black magic don't work on them and it don't work for them.

The black art, sorcery, and black magic only work when nature is in agreement with them as a means of punishment. This is why they only have effect on people they are directed to harm when they are living against the law that govern life which make them to be of the same vibration with them.

We are created in the likeness of God, therefore we are superior to the power of life that stream through black art, sorcery, and black magic. Our mind contain the greatest energy and the energy of black art, sorcery, and black magic are of the lowest energy, it is our mind that animate them with life and our mind can also remove life from them.

As there are rules that guide everything in life, there are rules that guide the use of the power of thought which is the likeness of the power of God that dwell in everyone.

The first rule to obey is to strictly live in accord with the law that govern life for any law that we break will stand against directing our thought to a good purpose to be effective for a period of time, until the time expire, our thought will not be effective and because it take some time for this period to expire, people doubt which make their thought not to materialize.

The second rule is to strictly control what you think. You should be able to think one thought without thinking the opposite thought, which will diverged the thought and neutralize it.

Everything in life have their power but there is no power that equal the power of thought when it is directed to fulfill a purpose which is faith.

It may sound simple, the power of a directed thought which is faith is the greatest power but this power cannot work without living a positive life which is why faith don't work for many people and some people are not patient enough to wait for faith to work because they doubt which is also faith, a directed thought that say it will not work.

Life originate from the law which manifest as God and it is the mind of God which is the image of God that our mind was created in it likeness. We therefore possess the power of God which manifest in us as faith, which is a directed thought to fulfill a purpose.

In the story of the tower of Babel, when the people come together to build a tower that will lead to heaven, God scatter the people knowing that when minds come together, they can achieve any purpose they strongly direct their mind to. This story is a figurative story that show the power of the mind. When minds become united, they generate a large force that can achieve anything that it is strongly aim at.

When the world was created, God think and speak his thought and everything start taking shape according to the thought of God. It is this likeness of God which is directing our thought that we were created in it form. Animals are not created in the likeness of God because they cannot direct their thought to fulfill a purpose. We human that are created in the likeness of God consider our thought to be trivial and put ourselves in the level of animal that are not in the likeness of God.

Those that want faith find it hard to have faith because they cannot think straight. They think one minute and doubt what they think the next minute and thereby cancel what they think with their doubt. Many people think to the right one second and redirect their thought to the left the next second, sometime becoming confused in thought thinking many things in a zigzag form.

To build spiritual power, you must learn to direct what you think and you must not allow your mind to think what you do not want to think.

Spiritual power is to be able to direct your thought to a purpose and see it through without doubt, and in the presence of obstacle, you must not become confuse because obstacle are meant to add strength to your inner strength.

The first thing God create on earth was light. When God said "let there be light", it took a thousand years for light to take form and God never doubted it but can we human wait as that long to see light take shape? Many of us will doubt it but if we can think and not doubt our thought, our thought will surely come to life if we can wait patiently for it to come to life when we are living a positive life.

You should not use force in directing your thought because using force work against the thought you are directing, force cause friction. Directing your thought with force is wanting to force your thought to work but you can never force your thought to work, your thought have it own energy which come from the positive life you are living and it work by itself. The energy that make your thought to work come from the law that govern life that you keep. Read the law that govern life again and master them because keeping the law that govern life is what that will give you everything you need in life.

Jesus said that if you have faith, you will move mountain but faith is believing your thought without force that the mountain will move.

What prevent many people form keeping their mind on a single thought to achieve a purpose is that their mind have taken to the shape of their condition. As they try to keep their mind in a particular thought to achieve a desired purpose, their present condition that their mind have taken to will be giving them doubt and drawing their mind to the shape of the condition that their present condition have taken to. For instance, if one is poor, the mind will take to the shape of poverty and if one is rich, the mind will take to the shape of wealth and if one is ill, the mind will take to the shape of the illness. Any condition that you are in, your mind will take to it shape and it is govern by your thought by your thinking of it. When you think the thought of your condition, it will be difficult for you to direct the faith that will bring you out of your condition. Instead of you to think of your condition think the way out of your condition and if you persist, a way will be shown to you.

To keep the mind on a purpose will be hard or easy depending on your condition. Someone that is poor and ill will find it difficult to keep the mind on a purpose to achieve a desired result than the one that is only poor.

Whatever your condition is, if you can overcome the thought of the condition in your mind which is the shape that the condition have given your mind that is creating a force of attraction of the condition to your mind, within a period of time reality will reshape the condition and the condition will shape itself to the new thought you now have in your mind. For anyone to overcome this force, one have to be able to calm his or her mind. If you are poor, make your mind calm and direct it to the shape of a rich mind by thinking of what you can do that will bring you out of poverty to riches. The thought alone is not enough you must act along with the thought.

A contented rich person have a calm mind, you must make your mind calm before it can take the shape of a rich mind. You should be aware that your mind alone cannot bring you riches it is what you do with your mind that will bring you riches.

Directing your mind for one hour or one day cannot be of much effect. You must direct the thought of what you want continuously which is directing your mind till you get the desired result. If you can make your mind calm and you do not doubt that you will get what you want, with time depending on the fate that is standing against you and what you want, you will get what you want. When you doubt, you are unconsciously saying that you cannot get what you want.

Directing our mind to what we want is to keep the picture of what we want in our mind. We think in picture, not in words, so do not direct your thought in words, direct it in picture.

When we direct our thought in words, it mean that we are creating fantasy. It take energy to direct our thought in words but it did not take energy to direct our thought in picture. If you are becoming tired of directing your thought, know that you are directing your thought in words.

To have faith is to believe and to believe is to accept in your mind that what you want will become reality. With this, you are to hold what you want in your mind that it will become a reality which is holding the picture of what you want in your mind.

Many people think that physical weakness is responsible for their present state. Physical weakness is not responsible for any condition, it is mental weakness that is responsible for every bad condition and living a negative life is responsible for mental weakness.

For you to change your life, you need to change the way you are living your life which depend on the organization of your mind that depend on what you think.

You should not look at the state of your condition because looking at the state of your condition will animate your condition with life. You should not look at the state of the condition of another person because if you look at the state of another person's condition will influence you to look at the state of your condition. The state of your condition can easily make you think negative and prevent you in directing your mind to what you want.

Do not mentally accept any condition that you do not want. For you not to mentally accept any condition that you do not want, do not think of the condition that you do not want. It is idleness of the mind that attract negative thought, therefore do not dwell in idleness so that you will not have the time to think of your condition.

The fate that is against many people prevent them from directing their thought to achieve a purpose but everyone can use the power of thought against every odd if one strictly live a positive life.

Keeping the law that govern life will aid you in directing your thought while living against the law that govern life will prevent you from directing your thought to achieve a purpose.

Everything have it price and if you are not ready to pay the price of what you want, it will be difficult for you to get what you want. There is nothing that is free in life, anything you want, you must be ready to pay the price. Jesus is a powerful person but look at the strict life that he live. I believe that many people will like to be as powerful as Jesus but many of them will not like to live the strict life that Jesus live as the price for this power.

THE POINT OF POWER IN YOU

The brain is in two part, the cerebellum and the cerebrum. The cerebellum is the small back brain and it is subtle because it existence is not easily known.

The cerebrum is the large front brain that control every activity of the body and it is divided into two part, the right brain and the left brain and their activities are interwoven. The cerebrum control both conscious and the unconscious activity of the body.

The point of the connection of the power of life to the body is the cerebellum which in turn animate the cerebrum. Your cerebrum connect your cerebellum and your cerebellum connect God.

The cerebellum don't think and it don't analyze things, it only give power to the activity of the cerebrum. What that is in your cerebrum is what your cerebellum will give power to from the source of life which is life itself meaning that any thought that you persistently think is what life will give power to through your cerebellum.

The cerebellum act base on what that is stored in the cerebrum which impress itself on the cerebellum that shape it to reality.

You should remove every negative thought from your mind by not giving them attention and strictly command your attention so that no thought should impress itself on it for your cerebellum to act upon.

The cerebellum guide everyone that want to live a good life through conscience. It speak silently to warn you when you are about to do something wrong but after it have warn you for some time and you persist in doing wrong, it will stop to warn you and you will become dead in conscience which will make you to do something wrong without any remorse.

If you are living a good life and you are about to take a wrong step, your cerebellum will warn you in a small voice. It don't argue and it don't give reason, it simply tell you to do or not to do and keep silent for you to decide what step to take and experience will tell you that the small voice is always right because the cerebellum connect to God that is all knowledge.

It is the cerebellum that speak to us through dream in figure of speech. Because the cerebellum did not learn language for it is universal in nature. It speak to us through what we store in our cerebrum.

Because dreams are in figure of speech make some dream to be difficult to understand although some people are fortunate that their dreams are not in figure of speech which make their dream easy to understand.

Some people did not believe dream because their dreams are too odd in figure of speech which need an interpretation from a gifted one in interpreting dreams similar to the case of King Pharaoh that have two dreams in figure of speech that was too difficult for anyone to interpret except Joseph, the gifted one in interpreting dreams.

If you can become virtuous to the point that you can know what you want to know through your cerebellum, you will understand what many people consider to be mystery and your cerebellum will be able to guide you through life.

You must be careful not to confuse your cerebellum and your imagination because your imagination can take form and speak to you. The difference between your cerebellum and your imagination in speaking to you is that your imagination will keep speaking to you while your cerebellum will speak to you in a small voice.

A saint direct the cerebellum positively through living a moral life while a sinner direct the cerebellum negatively through living an immoral life. The major difference between a saint and a sinner is that a saint control his or her mind while a sinner allow his or her mind to control him or her. Another major difference between a saint and a sinner is that a saint avoid the range of sin while a sinner dwell within the range of sin.

A saint don't walk on the land that angel fear to thread but a sinner don't mind sleeping on the land that angel fear to thread because you cannot walk on a muddy ground without your feet getting muddy.

When you persistently think a thought, the thought will impress itself on the cerebellum and the cerebellum will impress the thought on the omnipotent power to become real. The thought will start taking shape and impress itself on nature which will rearrange nature to shape itself according to the thought and it will become a reality.

Why many people are not able to bring their thought to reality and are not able to exercise faith is that they become discourage if it take long for their thought to materialize. Fate bring friction to our thought to materialize when it is negative and aid our thought to materialize when it is positive. Negative fate can be overcome if we persist in bringing our thought to reality.

Thought is faith in action and if anyone can hold his or her thought long enough, even if it take years, it will materialize.

You cannot force your thought to work, it work by itself, you only need to direct your mind to the reality of your thought till it materialize. You don't have to be idle waiting for your thought to materialize, you have to be doing something that will lead to the reality of your thought and you must live a virtuous life that will aid your thought to become a reality

You need to persistently direct your thought without doubt and be patient with it because your thought will materialize at its own time, not your own time because your thought will work according to your fate. Delay come when your thought have to contend with your fate.

The desire for mental gratification and the desire for gratification of the senses have downward pull of the mind to matter. If we cannot control the desire for gratification of the senses, the desire may attract our mind to negativity that will darken the mind to the cerebellum to have positive effect on it.

The cerebrum have downward pull of the mind to matter which are transient and the cerebellum have the upward pull of the mind to God. Living a positive life pull the mind to the light, to it salvation.

It is because of the power that the cerebellum gives to our thought that make King Solomon to tell everyone to guard their heart (mind) with all vigilant because out of it are the source of life. King Solomon said this because any thought that we think, whether for ourselves or for another person the cerebellum will act upon to manifest and reward us if it is a good thought or punish us if it is a bad thought. The cerebellum don't select thought, it simply act on any thought that we continuously think.

Many religion use fasting to break the downward pull of the mind to matter so that they can be connected to the cerebellum where they can find God. Some religion abstain from some type of food so that they can loose the grip of the mind to matter and be connected to their cerebellum consciously where they can find God.

Directing what you think is directing the power of God that stream through you. Any thought that you persistently direct your mind to, the omnipotent power of God that dwell in your cerebellum will act upon and the effect will fall back on you be it good to uplift you and be it evil to suppress you.

The cerebellum don't reason whether one thought is good for you or the other thought is bad for you, it simply act on any thought that you continuously think be it good or evil that you did not latter think against.

The power of God will not prevent anyone from the misuse of it but it will punish anyone for the misuse of it.

Jesus said that the pure in heart (mind) will see God, if you can become pure in mind, you will see the God that dwell in you.

As you feed your mind with conscious thought, unconscious thought may enter your mind without you inviting it which can lead to conscious thought. You must be attentive in your thinking as you are attentive when driving because if you lose your attention, it can lead to hazard.

Think straight; do not think in a zigzag form. Do not think one thought and think another against it because if you think one thought and think another thought against it, it will neutralize it. When you think in a zigzag form your cerebellum will not have thought to act upon because before your cerebellum act on one thought, you have divert your mind to another thought that is not in line with your former thought.

Thinking an aimless thought will lead you to live an aimless life and many people are living this type of life thereby subjecting themselves to evil influence from the negative force.

When you think without directing your thought, your mind will become open to another mind to pass through to your cerebellum and impress your cerebellum to act on a thought, either to harm you, to heal you, or to bless you. Hypnotism is an act of directing and controlling another person's mind. Hypnotism work on people that cannot control their mind which make another person to hypnotize them.

The secret of mental healing is directing a healing thought to the person you want to heal and if the person accept the thought, healing will take place and mental healing easily work on children because they have no other thought to struggle against unlike adult that have many thought to struggle against. Miracle is similar to mental healing but it is different in the sense that you can get anything you want through miracle. Jesus turn water into wine and this is a miracle of the highest order similar to the act of creation by God.

The secret of performing miracle on another person is that when the person have faith in you and your mind is strong enough to penetrate the person's mind to get to the cerebellum for you to command it, the person's cerebellum will yield to your command if you have enough mental strength to command it.

When Jesus want to heal people that did not have faith, Jesus will ask them if they have faith that he can heal them so that the question can generate faith in the person. Having faith on the person that can heal you is to aid the person in the act of healing you and to open your mind to the healer so that the healer can get to your cerebellum to command it. In Jesus home town, Jesus was not able to perform many miracle because the people of the town did not have faith in him because he grew up among them.

If you can be mentally calm, no form of psychic attack will have effect on you because if you are calm, your mind will be closed and the psychic attack will not have passage to your cerebellum to direct it and have effect on you.

You must understand that one good thought cannot change your life, it is continuous good thought that will change your life. As you continue to think good thought, speak good words and do good deed without interfering in the life of another person, your cerebellum will impress itself on nature to clear the obstacle that your past wrong thought and deed have laid before you and start to impress nature to rearrange itself to aid your progress. If you have create many obstacle to yourself through your bad thought and deed, it will take some time before nature can clear every obstacle that is standing against your progress before all your good thought can take effect. If the good you want seem to take long, do not be discourage for with time, nature will clear all the obstacle if you did not add additional obstacle through your thought and deed and all your good thought will take effect.

You should always remember that to direct your cerebellum to act on your thought to take effect, all you need to do is to hold the thought of what you want in your mind as you will see a picture in your mind. You are not to force your thought on what you want nor should you show your cerebellum the way you want it to be. Your cerebellum work on your thought by itself. If you try to force your thought on your cerebellum, it will be similar to trying to force God to do things for you.

Jesus said that if you have faith without doubt, you will receive anything you ask for and you may doubt when you think of how what you want will materialize. Do not think of how what you want will materialize, only hold the picture of what you want in your consciousness till it materialize. Doubt will always come when you look at the state of your condition but you should ignore the doubt and focus on what you want.

The human mind have been programme by the environment from childhood which make it difficult for the mind to remain calm and have faith without doubt. Everyone can break from this environmental influence by continuously directing the mind to only good thought when the mind need to be directed and remain calm when the mind need not to be directed. If anyone can achieve this, such one will be a spiritual giant.

THE BODY AND THE MIND

When the body is active, the mind will also become active to keep up with the active body because any effect of the body have effect on the mind and any effect of the mind have effect on the body.

If the body is active and the mind is not with the activity of the body, the mind will be thinking of the past or be on fantasy of the future so as to become active as the body is active. Direct your mind to keep up with the activity of the body by the focus of the mind on what the body is doing so that the mind and the body can be in harmony. If the mind and the body are in harmony, it will enhance perfection in what you are doing and you will work for a long time without getting tired.

If you are resting and you are not tired, your mind will start using the energy at your disposal to think of the past or to fantasize on the future because since your body is not using the energy, your mind will be using the energy which make idleness to be a kind of harm to our peaceful existence. Instead of to waste the energy on fantasy, you should calm yourself to conserve the energy. If you cannot be calm to conserve your energy, direct your energy to the way you want your life to be.

Sometime you can be full of energy and if your body cannot conserve the energy, your mind will use the energy to think various thought. You must not allow yourself to waste this energy, use this energy to propel faith and use it to direct your aim and purpose.

Every thought you think consume energy and if you don't direct your thought to what will favor your life, your mind will waste the energy on useless thought that may harm you.

If you are filled with energy and if there is no useful work to spend the energy on, preserve the energy with calmness by making your body and your mind to be calm. Energy that is spend in one direction cannot be available for another direction. If you spend your energy in a useless way, it will not be available for useful way.

If you have excess energy and you have free time, do not waste the energy and the free time on frivolous activity. Use your energy and free time to develop your life by reading good book that will add something positive to your life.

When you spend your energy in worldly activity that will yield nothing, you are spending your energy uselessly and it will not be available when you need the energy to add something to your life that will enhance your life. When you worry, fear, tense, and anxious, you are wasting your energy and you will also be creating resistance and friction to yourself but when you are calm and confident, you are conserving your energy and you will be able to analyze and solve difficult problem.

As a child learn to walk step by step, so you must learn to control your mind step by step till you are able to control it. The control of your mind lie the control of your energy.

Many people cannot control their mind because they think that the mind can be control in one minute. The mind cannot be control in one day, not even one week. The control of the mind is a gradual process till one become perfect in the control of the mind.

There is nobody that can control the mind when living a negative life, we must live a positive life before we can control our mind.

Sometime you may not have the desire to control your mind due to depression. Do not allow depression to come to you, charge yourself up when you are feeling depress by thinking of something that will make you feel alive.

It is the thought of doubt and fear that bring depression, do not permit these two thought to come close to your mind because they are the instrument of the negative force of trapping the mind to make it confuse.

Do not be excited because when you are excited, you will become open to mental influence and you may lose the control of the mind. When you are excited, your mind will become active and you will start to respond to what you see and hear which will make your mind difficult to control. Anytime you are excited, you must try as much as possible to calm yourself by dwelling in silence.

When you are excited, use your body to control your mind to become calm because the body and the mind have effect on each other. In the state of excitement, make your body to become relax by putting your body in a relax position and if you do this for some minute depending on the level of your excitement, your mind will become relax. If you are sitting, sit in the position of confidence to make your mind relax and if you are walking, walk slowly when in a state of excitement because excitement will make you to walk briskly. Look at the life of a king, a king don't walk briskly, a king walk slowly because a king do not get excited, he is always calm and you should be a king and live the life of a king.

Be a king and always be a king. A king don't exercise fear even if there is fear, a king give hope. A king is always peaceful even if everyone is troubled because a king don't have to lose his mind, always be a king and let your mind be under your control.

When your body is under your control, your mind will also be under your control but when you neglect to control your body, your mind will also be out of your control.

For you to understand the relationship between the body and the mind, study how a depress person sit and sit that way if you will not become depress and study how a happy confident person pose and pose that way if you will not become confident and happy.

The most important reason to keep the law that govern life is that any law that you keep will reflect in your behavior and every law that you break will also reflect in your behavior. A positive person will reflect a positive behavior and a negative person will reflect a negative behavior. Study how a thief behave. If you look at a thief straight in the eyes, the thief will blink his or her eyes and turn away his or her face, a gesture that show that the thief is trying to hide his or her mind from you. And if you look at a blameless person straight in the eyes, the blameless person will return the gaze and if the blameless is the shy type, the blameless person will look down, a gesture that show shyness.

When you live against the law that govern life, you will possess a form of fear or should I say a form of fear will possess you. There will be a type of fear that will be tormenting you from time to time. If you strictly live in accord with the law that govern life, you will be confident to life and you will not be afraid of anything, not even death that nearly every person are afraid of.

You will lose the control of your mind and life if you are living a negative life and you will be in control of your mind and life if you are living a positive life. Do not think negative of another person because if you do, it will attract negativity to you.

When you hear negative talk and you accept it, the negative talk will register in your mind and your mind will generate negative thought out of it. The negative thought will attract more negative thought to your mind which will make you to act negatively whether consciously or unconsciously. When people are talking negatively, leave the place immediately and if you cannot leave the place immediately, do not accept the negative talk into your mind. Engage your mind with something positive so that the negative talk will not find entrance to your mind or you rephrase the negative talk to become positive in your mind.

To be director of your life, you must be confident and calm and you should strive to remain calm and confident at all time. When you are calm and confident, you will be able to direct your thought to what you are doing at the moment and you will also be able to direct your mind to whatever direction you want to direct it to.

To stay calm and confident, you should engage your mind in the thought of what is useful and be in mental silence if you are not engaging your mind in anything that is useful. You must always engage your mind in anything that you are doing. You should not be doing one thing and be thinking of another thing. Let whatever you are doing be in harmony with your thought. As you are doing one thing and engaging your mind in it, another thought will always want to gain entrance to your mind, you must not accept it, ignore it and it will go away by itself.

If you live in accord with the law that govern life, your mind will become your servant that will be obedient to you but if you live against the law that govern life, your mind will become your master that will dominate and control you.

Living in accord with the law that govern life will make your mind to lead you to your salvation but living against the law that govern life will make your mind to lead you to your destruction.

You are what you think and directing your thought is directing your life. Do not permit yourself to think what you do not want because thinking what you do not want will create a force within you that will make you unconsciously do what you do not want.

Keep directing your thought to what you want till they start to manifest in your life. If you cannot keep directing your thought to what you want which take concentration, other thought will create a force within you that will make you to unconsciously think what you don't want that will lead to conscious thought that will lead you to what you don't want.

If you want bliss, continue to think bliss and act bliss and with time, your life will become blissful but if you think the opposite whether consciously or unconsciously, that is what your life will become. Whichever you embrace will either make you able to control your mind or will make your mind to control you and if you allow your mind to control you, you are heading toward destruction.

PART 3

THE RELATIVE KNOWLEDGE

FATE

7

With the measure that you measure out it will be measure back to you – Jesus

DESTINY

Some people believe in destiny while some don't believe in destiny. Some people that believe in destiny believe that destiny can be change while some people that believe in destiny believe that destiny cannot be change. Whatever you believe in, you will belong to one of those category.

Destiny is the synonym of fate and it is one of the foundation that life was created.

Anything you give out will surely come back to you, any action that you take, there is an opposite reaction. Anything you give to life, within a period of time, life will give it back to you and this is your destiny, it is your fate.

If you live by the sword, you will surely die by the sword and the dying by the sword is the fate you create to yourself through living by the sword which make you destine to die by the sword.

Everything you do is what you cause to be and you will experience the reaction which is the effect of what you cause to be. Sometime the effect of what you cause to be may come upon you immediately or it may take a period of time before you experience the effect of what you cause to be and the longer it take for you to experience the effect, the bigger or more severe the effect will be on you. This is similar to the money you put in a bank to yield interest and the longer the money stay with the bank, the bigger your interest will be.

The only time you have power over fate is before you take the decision to do or not to do. Immediately you take a decision, before you carry out your decision, fate will start to arrange how to reward you if your decision is toward good or how to punish you if your decision is toward evil.

The atonement of wrong doing start from thought to the end result which is deed, so also is your right doing.

Science say that in every action, there are equal and opposite reaction. This have to do with the material plane, it is different in the spiritual plane. In the spiritual plane, every action yield multiple reaction.

Many people think that when they commit an act, the same act will be done back to them. It is not the same act but a multiple of the act or a big form of the act that will be done back to them except if the act is an act that is committed by mistake which will make it be exactly the same act that will be done back to them because the act did not originate from the mind.

Act are of two types which are meditated act and impulse act. A meditated act is the act that you plan before you do while an impulse act is the act that you did not plan before you do which you did not determine to do. A meditated act yield multiple reaction while an impulse act yield the same reaction.

You can determine how you will commit an act but the reaction or the atonement of the act is beyond your determination and you have no say on how fate will reward or punish you.

When one commit an act by mistake, many people think that the act committed by mistake will not bring atonement because it was not intentionally committed. Consider what make Jesus say that we must be perfect as our heavenly father is perfect – Matthew chapter 5 verse 48. It is a must that we live a good life and mistake is not allowed in the school of life which is why only the few will be chosen as said by Jesus. Everyone will atone for every deed whether by mistake or not, they only have different atonement.

It is a perfect being that don't do anything wrong but it is not easy to come to perfection. Perfection is base on the level of our experience and exposure to different people which will bring the understanding of how people act and react which suppose to make us know what to do and what not to do and what not to say and what to say at the right time without hurting anyone.

Those that live in seclusion or monastery because of perfection so as to avoid doing wrong to anyone by mistake will not be experience to being diplomatic with people and will not understand much of human nature. Living a perfect life that many people consider impossible depend on the level of experience to human relation and the level of exposure to how people act and react.

When you have learn to govern your emotion, you must learn not to set on the emotion of another person. You should always act in a way that the person that have become emotional should become calm.

If you commit an act, the act will go with you anywhere you go demanding for atonement anywhere there is the opportunity to atone for the act. As you atone for your act one after the other, you will become free from the obstacle that hinder your progress and you will gain spiritual freedom which is the essence of life.

Fate is the ruler of life that life designate it rulership to. If you do good, fate will give you good and if you do evil, fate will give you evil.

Some people may be doing evil and prosper in the midst of the evil which make it seem that the evil they are doing is giving them prosperity. The prosperity that anyone have at the time of doing evil is due to the good the person have done in the past and the time will come when the person will suffer for the evil he or she is doing now. If you are harvesting beans at the time of sowing rice did not mean that the rice have grown to yield beans, a time to reap the rice you are now sowing will come.

Everything operate in a circle. The sowing is the beginning of a circle and the reaping is the closing of the circle. As a circle start from a point to return to

the point it started from, every human affair start from a point to return to the point it started from.
The point that an act start from is the mind, from the thought in the mind it proceed to act either to create or to destroy and it return to the mind which is the starting point to lead to the salvation or destruction of the person.

Let us look at some example of the circle of act from the Bible. Jacob deceive his father Isaac by pretending to be Esau, his twin brother so as to get the blessing meant for Esau from their father Isaac which Jacob succeed in getting. After some period of time, Jacob married and gave birth to many children. Jacob develop likeness for one of his son more than the rest of them. Joseph was loved more than his brothers which make his brothers to become jealous of him, at a time, Joseph had a dream that was interpreted that all his brothers will bow to him. At another time, Joseph had another dream that was interpreted that all his brothers including their parent will bow down to him. These two dreams increase the jealousy that Joseph's brothers have against him which make them gang and sell Joseph to a trader and deceive their father that a wild beast have devour Joseph. The lie that Jacob lied to his father Isaac was harmless to Isaac but the atonement of the lie that Jacob lied to his father Isaac which was the lie that his children conspire to lie to him was extremely harmful to Jacob.

Many people think that God will forgive them because God is a merciful God. If they beg for mercy, God will forgive them because God is a merciful God. It is true that God will forgive them for them to continue their relationship with God but they will have to atone for the crime because atonement is one of the foundation that life was erected and there is no one that can change a foundation unless the person want to collapse the structure.

Let us consider the case of Prophet Elijah that atone for his slaughter of the prophet of Baal in another life time. Something that is negative is negative whether one do it for God or for any other reason and to kill is extremely negative.
In the lifetime of Prophet Elijah, he did not atone for the slaughter of the prophet of Baal because he was too powerful for anyone to kill him, he did not taste death but ascend to heaven – 2 King chapter 2, verse 11. Prophet Elijah reincarnated as meek John to prepare the way for the mission of Christ and also to atone for the slaughter of the prophet of Baal by Herod that behead him. Nothing happen by chance, there is reason behind everything that happen in life. Jesus said that a leaf will not fall from a tree without the knowledge of God which mean that God is aware of everything that happen to everyone and atonement is the order of God.

Let us consider the case of Apostle Paul that so much preach grace as the forgiveness of sin and that the grace of Jesus Christ have wash away the sin of every repented Christian. Before Apostle Paul who was formerly Saul become converted, he was seriously fighting against the disciples of Jesus but after his conversion, Apostle Paul paid for every sin that he committed against the follower of Jesus. If there is forgiveness of sin, he will not have paid for every sin that he committed against those following Jesus. Jesus appear in vision to Ananias and told him that Apostle Paul who was then Saul will suffer so many things for the sake of his name that he was fighting against.

Let us consider the case of Jesus Christ that died a horrible death on the cross of Calvary. Have you ever consider how painful it is for a person to be nailed to cross in the sun and allow to dry to death in the hot sun by dying slowly. Jesus said that the law of God cannot be annul and that everyone will reap what they sow. Jesus took the sin of the people that he heal upon himself. The lame walk, the blind see, a he raise the dead because he took their sin upon himself and he command them not to sin again so that something worst will not happen to them.

Every sin that a person commit bring a form of affliction or lack in the life of the sinner as the atonement for the sin and to take away the affliction mean that one will have to take the sin that bring the affliction. Since Jesus took the sin of the people that he heal upon himself and heal them of their affliction warrant him the horrible death on the cross as the atonement of the sin of the people he took upon himself.

The teaching of Peter, James and John, the closest disciple to Jesus lay much emphasis on sin that it is sin that bring pain, affliction and finally death and to remove pain, affliction and death, one have to stay away from sin that bring them.

Every sin have a proper time for it atonement and if it is not time for the atonement of any sin, provision will not be made for the atonement of the sin. If the people that Jesus heal did not deserve to be healed by Jesus, they will not have met Jesus for their healing to take place and for the atonement of their sin to be taken upon himself by Jesus.

Many people think that a trivial act did not count but as one continue to commit these little sin that people call trivial, they accumulate and become big sin that demand big atonement. If water continue to drip in a point, within a period of time, the dripping water will turn a pool of water. Do not consider anything to be trivial; there is nothing that is trivial before fate. If you are living a trivial life, you will become trivial and you will be attracted to trivial people.

Some people may think that they can run away from their fate. Everything you do, whether consciously or unconsciously will lead you to your fate. If you refuse to take a step because you are afraid that the step will lead you to your fate, the refusal to take the step will lead you to another step that will lead you to your fate.

What should you do if fate is against you? King Solomon said that calmness will lay many offense to rest. When you are calm to any situation, the calmness will reduce the spiritual effect of the situation. If the spiritual effect become reduce, the physical effect will also reduce because it is the spiritual that control the physical. If the effect of a situation is taken out of your psyche, you will see clearly to find your way out of the situation. This is the importance of meditation, an act of calming the mind.

When you are calm, you will see things the way they are but when you are nervous, you will exaggerate the situation and you will see it to be complex. The more fearful you are of a situation, the more complex the situation will appear. Fear is base on the negative imagination of a situation. We are afraid of the dark because we have negative imagination of the dark but if we can bring light to the dark, we will see that there is nothing in the dark that bring fear.

Do not harbor the thought that somebody is responsible for your situation because if you do, it will be similar to adding fuel to fire which will make the fire burn more. It is always tempting to want to see that someone is responsible for your situation but if fate want to punish you, fate itself will not punish you, it will use someone to punish you which will make it seem that it is the person that is punishing you. It is not the person that is punishing you, it is fate that is using the person to punish you. Jesus know from a point of time that Judas will betray him but he did not question Judas nor did he stop Judas to be one of his disciple because Jesus know that Judas is the means to the payment of the sin of the people that he took upon himself. Who will have betray Jesus to the ruling council if Jesus have stop Judas to be one of his disciple. It was not Judas that betray Jesus, it was fate that use Judas to betray Jesus and Judas also pay for allowing fate to use him to betray Jesus and Jesus understand it which make Jesus not to speak anything against Judas.

GOOD AND EVIL TIME

When you do a good deed, the good deed will form protection on you from evil for a period of time and until this time expire, no form of evil will come to you. The time may be long or it may be short depending on the type of good that you have done.

If you do an evil deed, the evil deed will prevent good form coming to you for a period of time, depending on the type of evil that you have done which will make the time to be long or to be short and until this time expire, no form of good will come to you.

If you see a person that you consider to be evil to be enjoying a good time, it mean that the person is enjoying the good that the person have done in the past, an evil time is awaiting the person in the future like a criminal that is awaiting trial. Since light and darkness cannot dwell in the same place at the same time, a person cannot enjoy a good time along with an evil time, one will have to wait for the other.

Consider the life of a thief. There are some thief that don't steal anything that belong to a poor person, they focus on stealing from only the rich and they sometime give to the poor. You cannot compare this type of thief with a thief

that steal from every person because the former thief will enjoy a measure of good than the thief that steal from every person but will also pay for his or her evil.
There are some assassin that judge the case of a person they are paid to kill whether the person they are paid to kill deserve to die and if the person did not deserve to die, they will not kill the person even if you give them all the money in the world. Compare this assassin with another assassin that kill any person he or she is paid to kill. The two assassin will pay for their evil but the former assassin will enjoy a measure of good.
I cite these two examples for everyone to see the reason why some people we consider to be evil enjoy some good that make it seem as if the evil is bringing them good.

When a child is born, if there is no serious fate that come to life with the child, the child will have the innocent face of a child. As the child continue to grow, if the parent of the child live a good life as example for the child to follow and if the child follow the good life, the face of the child will retain the innocent face of a child. If the child grow up to an adult and he or she maintain the good life that he or she grow up with, as an adult, he or she will retain the innocent face. When the child that have become an adult start to follow a particular path in life, the mind of the adult child will take to the shape and form of the path he or she is following. If the path is positive, his or her organ will function well which make him or her to have youthful vigor but if the path is negative, his or her body organ will not function well which will make him or her to lose youthful vigor. As he or she continue to incur fate, if the fate is positive, the fate will continue to uplift him or her. Anyone that can remain innocent throughout his or her lifetime will retain smooth innocent face till his or her death.

It is the mind of God that shape life and since we are created in the likeness of God, it is our mind that shape our body and our life. Everything about our life originate from our mind which is the instrument of shaping our life.

For you to live a positive life that have power over negative fate, do not see what you don't want to see in your life in the life of another person. If you are seeing what you don't want in your life in the life of another person, your mind will unconsciously pick it and attract it to your life without your conscious knowing it till it will start to manifest in your life sometime in the same form or in a different form.
It is anger, jealousy, greed, and lust that easily bind one to negative fate, you must strictly guard your mind against these vice.

Do not have the thought that one person is your enemy. If you have the thought of enemity toward any person, the thought of enemity will hamper your progress and another person will have the same thought toward you. It is the negativity in you that attract negativity from another person to you. To be

negative is evil and it will attract evil from another person to you to harm you and beside this, there is not form of evil that can harm you.
If you think evil or you permit any form of negativity to dwell in you, you are giving evil people power to have dominion over you and the more you think or do evil, the more evil people will have dominion over you.

If you think only good thought and you continue to do good deed, the good in you will dispel every evil around you like light that make every form of darkness disappear.
To rise above your present situation, you should not be disgusted with it nor should you pity yourself because of it. Accept any situation the way they are and see it as a condition you must overcome because your present is the step that will lead to your future and if you run away from your present, you are running away from the step that will lead you to your future. Every situation you are passing through is meant to teach you and you attract it to yourself through fate and not until you learn and apply the lesson that you will rise above the fate.

THE

WAY

OF

PRAYER

8

Keep on asking and it will be given you, keep on seeking and you will find, keep on knocking and it will be open to you – Jesus

THE ACT OF PRAYER

Good is light and evil is darkness. If you are one step away from good, it mean that you are one step to evil and if you are many step away from good, then you are many steps to evil for the absent of good mean the present of evil.

The more distant you are from good, the more distance you will be from God and the distance it will be for God to hear your prayer. This is similar to calling someone from a far distant and the farther the distance, the difficult it will be for the person you are calling to hear you. This did not mean that God is far away from you, it is you that is far away from God. Evil cast distance on the path of the one that indulge in evil which make the one that indulge in evil to be far away from God.

The closer you are to God which is the level of good in you, the faster will your prayer be answered but the farther you are away from God which is the level of evil in you, the slower will your prayer be answered. If you are living a positive life which mean that you are dwelling in the light, everything you need will meet you at the right time before you ask for it.

Our thought when directed is faith. Prayer is speaking our thought to God and when we speak our thought without faith will be similar to a plate without food but faith without living a positive life lead to nothing.

When you pray, you must let your prayer harmonize with your thought and let your life harmonize with living a positive life that will give energy to your prayer. The power of your prayer lie in your thought and the power in your thought lie in the good life you are living. If you are living a bad life, there will be no energy in your thought that will make your prayer to be effective.

You should not doubt that your prayer may not come true. If doubt come to your mind, it is because you are thinking whether your prayer will come true or not. Direct your thought to what you are praying for by believing in what you are praying for till it come to reality. Remember the story of Joseph that pass through jealousy, through servitude, and through prison before his dream which was his prayer come true and he never doubted his dream.

Some prayer take long to manifest. There are two reasons for this. The first reason is that nature will have to rearrange itself for your prayer to come true and the second reason is that you have to pass through some rigor as a form of training to become what you are praying for. The rigor that you will pass through which may bring delay to your prayer is to develop your inner strength. Joseph pass through jealousy in order to develop the inner strength to resist jealousy and respond wisely when he become the king of another nation so that he can preserve the life of many people. Joseph pass through seduction to test him if he can continue with the journey that will lead him to be a king and if he had succumb to the seduction, he will never have been taken to the prison where they keep the king prisoner which lead him to interpreting dreams that led him to the king. In the house of Portiphar, Joseph positive character make him superior to other slave which make Portiphar and his wife to like him and in the prison, his positive character make the prison ward not to place restriction on him.

It is the way that you live your life that will determine whether your prayer will come true or not.

If you want something in your life, whether you pray a verbal prayer for it or not, you must act in line with what you want and you must remain positive in character. Your action toward what you want must portray expectancy and with this, you will keep your prayer and what you want alive.

When some people pray, they forget what they have pray for until they realize that their prayer have not yield result. If you are praying for money to live a good life and not to satisfy your ego and pride, you must not act as if you will not get the money. Act as if you will get the money you are praying for because if your action portray that you will not get the money you are praying for, it can bring resistance to your prayer.

If you are sick and you have money to treat yourself, it is not advisable to depend on your prayer to heal you. You are to go to the medical people to take care of your health because spending money on your health can be a form of atonement. But if you are sick and you did not have money to take care of your health or if the sickness did not have a medical solution, you have no choice than to develop the faith that will heal you. You must develop the mental strength to direct your mind to the thought of getting well even if there seem to be no hope, you must direct your mind to the hope that you will get well even if it take long for you to get well. If you can persistently believe and you believe long enough when you are living a positive life, you will become well.

You must always remember that directing your thought which is faith will not work and your prayer will not work if you are living against the law that govern life.

Apostle James said that faith without work is dead. What this mean is that faith will not work when living against the law that govern life for to live against the law that govern life is to live against faith.

FAITH

Faith is to believe but our believe must be base on reason. There is no one that can prove the existence of God but there is every reason to believe in God.

To have faith without reason is useless, there must be a reason to have faith. When you have faith, doubt will come when your reason is not strong enough to back your faith.
Those that say there is no God did not have any reason to believe that there is God. If anyone is able to convince them with a reasonable reason that there is God and if the reason can lead them to experience the feeling that there is God, they will believe in God because God is a personal experience, it is not a general experience.

All petty argument that we argue about life lead to hostile feeling which bring petty quarrel that close the mind of the other person concerning faith and also blindfold us and lead us away from God by not making our faith to be effective and are harmful to our prayer. Apostle Paul said that we should avoid argument because argument lead to nothing but hostility.
If someone say there is no God will not have effect on you and you saying there is God will not have effect on someone that strongly believe that there is no God. If you tolerate the other persons belief, the other person will tolerate your belief but if you find it difficult to tolerate the other person's belief, the other person will also find it difficult to tolerate your belief.

Your prayer and your faith will work depending on the fate that is binding you and standing against your prayer but if you can persist in faith long enough, your faith will overcome your fate.
Seek peace with all life; have nothing against anyone and do not do anything negative that will make anyone to have something against you.
Jesus said that if you bring your gift to the altar and you remember that your brother have something against you, leave your gift and go to your brother and make peace with your brother before you offer your gift to God. If you can live by this rule and make peace with everybody, your prayer will be effective.

Sometime prayer of faith get delay so that nature can rearrange itself for the prayer to come true. Let us assume that you are working in a branch of a bank and your position in the branch of the bank it next to the branch manager of the bank and you are praying to be a branch manager. Nature will not remove a branch manager for you to occupy the position unless if a branch manager is working against the rule of the bank. For your prayer to become a reality, nature may make the bank to expand and create a new branch that you will be made it manager or nature may create room for the promotion of a branch manager that deserve promotion so as to create space for you to be a branch manager and it will take time because it cannot happen overnight.

Anger is a big obstacle to prayer and many people did not realize this. Any form of anger you harbor will bring resistance to your prayer. If you continue to make people happy, it will speed up your prayer and if you live peacefully with everyone be it a saint or a sinner will give your prayer a great lift.

You should not pray against the free will of another person because you are not in the authority to decide what is good for the other person. What you think is good for the other because you think it is good for you may harm the other person that you think is good for. For instance, if one person want to be a doctor and you are praying that the person should be a lawyer, you are praying against the free will of this person.

Your faith depend on the level of your purity. You must be pure in mind by not having anything against anyone and you must live your life in a way that will make anyone not to have something against you. Live at peace with everyone which will add strength to your faith.

Form the habit of giving whenever anyone ask something from you so as to make people happy which will boost your prayer but if you give out of pride will not boost your prayer. This did not mean that you will be searching for who to give, you should only give whenever there is opportunity to give. Your aim in giving is to make people happy and if someone did not want your gift, your gift will not make the person happy. The greater the happiness your gift give to people, the greater will be your reward through what you are praying for.

You should not create fantasy over what you are praying for. Fantasy make the mind weak and if your mind is weak, your faith will be weak because your faith depend on the strength of your mind.

If you think a single thought, the thought will be strong but if you direct different thought to the single thought, the different thought will not be strong but will be weak.

Everyone needs calmness of the mind to generate faith because faith cannot be generated in a troubled mind.

Faith and calmness is similar to a principle in mechanic which state that for energy to be utilize, it must be stored so that it can be directed. If you are clam, you are storing your energy and when you have faith, you are directing your stored energy. If you are not calm, you will not have energy to propel your faith. A disturb mind cannot direct thought and directing thought is faith. Prayer without faith is a river without water and a river without water is not a river, it is a drainage.

TYPES OF PRAYER

Prayer is an act of directing our thought to a superior power but to pray without having faith in oneself is against reason and such prayer will not be effective. For instance, if you are praying to pass exam when you did not prepare yourself for the exam by reading is against reason. You must read so as to pass your exam and you can pray for you to remember what you read so that you can pass your exam. If you prepare yourself for an exam and you have faith in yourself that you will pass the exam because you understand everything you read, you don't need luck, you will only pray for luck when you don't prepare yourself for the exam.

The type of prayer that people pray depend on the religion they belong. The highest authority in life is the intelligence that create life and this intelligence came out of the law and any person that live by the law will be connected to this intelligence.

There are gods that head every religion but it is assume that the creator is jealous of these gods, but can the creator be jealous of the created? If the creator is jealous of the created, it means that the creator and the created are of the same range of power which is not possible.

God create human and human create machine. One can then say that human was form according to the mind of God and machine was form according to the mind of man. Have the best of machine ever been jealous by the lowest of mankind. If the lowest human cannot be jealous of machine then God cannot jealous the gods worship by human. Jealousy is human characteristic, God cannot be jealous of any other being.

Every machine reflect the mind of man, if man cease to exist, every machine will also cease to exist. Every human and every being reflect the mind of God and if God cease to exist, every human will also cease to exist so also every being. If human cease to exist, everything in creation will cease to exist because human is the apex of creation.

There are hierarchy in the gods that head every religion. There are higher gods that did not have any relation with human and there are lower gods that are in the same level with human and there are gods that are lower than the human level. The problem with human is that they don't realize the god that they are which make them to worship the gods that are on the same level with them and worship the god that is lower than them. Human can only realize the god that they are if they can direct their thought and they can only direct their thought if they live in accord with the law that govern life.

Jealousy is the characteristic of an immature mind, it cannot be seen in a matured mind. Jealousy cannot be seen among the gods for a lower god have honor for a higher god and a higher god understand the low level of a lower god.

All the gods that people consider to be fiction are real but most of them are lower than the present human state. Their days of importance was when the human mental state was low but now they are nothing to the modern man. The people that worship low god are wasting their time.

All the higher gods are the messenger of light and we call them god because of their supernatural power and all the lower gods are the messenger of darkness and they will lead everyone that succumb to them to darkness, their own destruction.

It was Angel Gabriel that appear to Mary that she will be pregnant with the pregnancy of Jesus that also appear to Mohammed and speak the Holy Quran to him in a cave. Jesus Christ is the beginning of Christianity and Mohammed is the beginning of Islam.

Different prayer are associated with different religion which originate from the head of the religion.

Every form of prayer need faith in the prayer for the prayer to work and if one did not have faith in the prayer, the prayer may not work. We can therefore say that it is not the prayer that is working, it is your faith in the prayer that is working which lie in your thought.

The prayer of some religion is chanting while that of some is meditation. What many people consider to be prayer is speaking their thought to God and since it is our thought that generate every form of prayer, what type of thought that we think be it good or evil is a request to life that life will grant if we persist in it therefore every thought that we think is a prayer for good or a prayer for evil.

Apostle Paul said that we should pray without ceasing and to pray without ceasing is to continuously direct our thought to what we want which is to continue to believe what we want which is faith.

Doubt which is a strong enemy of faith always come through the influence of the environment. What people generally believe have influence on each other and you should summon the inner strength to overcome this environmental influence.

Jesus said that if you have faith like a mustard seed, you can move mountain and a mustard seed is a small seed. If you can summon the strength to believe in the midst of your doubt, your prayer will bring result. It is the law of life that guide everything in life, if you are living against the law of life you will not be able to summon the strength to believe in the midst of doubt.

Many people believe in the law of Moses which state that an eye for an eye, a tooth for a tooth, and a blow for a blow. If you believe in this law and somebody blow you and you blow the person back, you will be the same as the person that blow you and both of you will be law breaker. Any law that you break will stand against your prayer depending on the law you break.

Do good to everyone in the midst of any evil they have done to you. If you can persevere in doing good, you will have the strength to build your mental strength.

Anything that you do, be it to a friend or a foe with either be for your prayer to come true or will be against your prayer.

Many people think that an evil person is responsible for their problem and it can be true but the fact is that the present of darkness mean the absent of light because if good which is God dwell in you, evil cannot come to you because no darkness can come near light. Job went through a lot of evil close to the point of death and he did not blame anyone for it because he know that the present of darkness is the absent of light and he also know that this world is a world of duality, a world where good and evil exist side by side. Because Job dwell in the light, the light in him later dispel the darkness and God bless his end more than his beginning.

If there is evil in your life and you resist the evil, the evil will persist because your resistance to the evil will give the evil strength to persist. If there is evil in your life, find the reason behind the evil and if you remove the reason behind the evil, the evil will go away by itself. The reason behind evil is evil itself and evil polish us to become good for we to abstain from doing evil.

Our thought have energy of their own to make things happen and this is the major lesson we have to learn from evil for if we think evil, either to ourselves or to another person, our thought will attract evil to us. A lot of people consider thought to be nothing. Whether you believe thought to be nothing or not, your life spring from your thought. The essence of verbal prayer is to add power to your thought because the words that we speak have energy of their own that is different from the energy of the thought that we think.

Whether you direct your prayer to God or you use the power of your mind to direct your thought to what you want, the most important point is to believe in yourself and the indwelling ability in you which is the power of faith which lie in your thought. Do not consider this to be trivial, anything you will be in life depend on what you think of yourself and not what another person think of you whether the person is evil or not.

Since faith lie in your thought, any thought that you think, you are generating faith to the good in your life or to the evil in your life. If you think destructively, you are generating faith that will destroy your life and if you think constructively, you are generating faith that will construct your life.

With every thought that you think, every word that you speak and every deed that you do, a measure of good will be added to you or a measure of good will be subtracted from you.

Anything that you do to another person, you do to yourself. The major training we are to undergo in life is to live for the other person and by living for the other person, we are living for ourselves.

All the laws that govern life is to live for God and we live for God by living for our neighbor because if we live for God, we will live for our neighbor and if we live for our neighbor, we are living for ourselves.

When more than two people agree on something, each of the people are adding mental strength to what they agree upon which will make what they agree upon to have great force. If it is a collective prayer, the prayer will have great force to achieve what it is directed at.

You must not do what that will make people to have negative impression of you because when people agree on something about you, the thing they agree upon will have hypnotic effect on you unless you have the mental strength to counter the hypnotic effect.

There are different types of spiritual forces which are the mental or thought force, the force of sorcery, the force of the black art and magic, and the force of witchcraft. People consider the mental force or the thought force to be the weakest spiritual force because it did not cost anything to think. This thought or mental force is the strongest spiritual force because there is no force that can outweigh faith, a directed thought to fulfill a purpose.

If you can persistently direct your thought to fulfill a purpose without doubt, there is no power that can equal it or obstruct it when you are living a positive life. If people come together to direct their thought to fulfill a purpose without doubt, each of the people will be adding mental strength to fulfill the purpose.

To defend yourself against any force that is directed at you is to remain calm in the presence of the force without reacting to it. If you can do this, the force will be reflected back to the sender because if you did not absolve energy, the energy will return to it starting point. To be calm is never to react to any thought in your mind, never to react to any word that you hear and never to react to anything that anyone do. This have to do with personal training and self development.

Do not accept anything that you do not want in the mental state which is your mind. If you are praying for anything and it seem that what you are praying for will not come true, do not accept it. Believe in what you are praying for till you realize it.

When you pray, do not be discourage if the prayer is not coming to reality because your discouragement can annul the prayer.

Prayers are annul due to living a negative life. It is important that we live a positive life but if you do something negative by mistake, do not condemn yourself. If you condemn yourself, the self crucifix will take form and stand against your faith. You need inner peace to manifest your prayer because sorrow, depression, chaotic mind, and hopelessness will delay and prolong what you are praying for.

THE SECRET OF TIME

9

Do not care about tomorrow, for tomorrow will care about itself, sufficient for each day is it own trouble – Jesus

THE REAL YOU

The now is the reality of time, time did not lie in the past and it did not lie in the future, time lie in what you do with the moment.

There is nothing that exist but the moment and when it have become the past, it no longer exist and when it is in the future, it is yet to exist. It is the moment that create the past and modify the future.

If you say tomorrow, next week, next month or next year you will start living a positive life, you may not live a positive life because the future is not the reality of time.

If you want to live a positive life, you must start to live the positive life now because nothing exist except in the moment. Anything that you want to achieve or anything that you want to be, you must start the achievement of it now and start to be what you want to be now for the future is not the reality of time.

Time is always the same, it only change it form and as time is always the same, everyone are always the same and they only change their form.

The real you always resist change except if you persistently make the real you to change through knowledge and knowing how to apply it.

Your body is not you, your soul is not you, and your spirit is not you. This is why you will say my body, my soul, my spirit. If your body is you, you will not say my body, if your soul is you, you will not say my soul, and if your spirit is you, you will not say my spirit. If they were you, you will not describe them as something belonging to you.

Your body is not you and your mind is not you but you cannot exist in an earth life without a body and a mind. You are what you do and you make use of your body and your mind to do what you do.

If you are a thief, it is the real you that is the thief. It is not your body that is the thief even though you use your body to carry out theft and it is not your mind that is the thief because you use your mind to plan theft. When people see that you are a thief, they will not say that it is your body that is the thief neither will they say that it is your mind that is the thief.

If you are a prostitute, you will not say that it is my body that is the prostitute even though you use your body for prostitution and you will not say that it is your mind that is the prostitute because you use your mind to enjoy prostitution.

The type of activity that you generate is what make the you to be you and not the instrument that you use to generate the activity which are your body and your mind.

Whatever you are is what you are and that is what you will be after death and that is what you will be reincarnated to be. Prophet Elijah was a great prophet in his former life and he was reincarnated as a great prophet to prepare the way for Jesus in another life. He was a celibate priest in his former life and was reincarnated as a celibate priest in another life in the days of Jesus Christ.

As time change it form and still remain the same, so you will change your form in the state called death and still remain the type of you that you are. If you are a thief before your death, you will remain a thief after your death and you will be reincarnated as a thief in your next earth life unless you change before your death or you undergo change in a most painful way after your death. If you are a prostitute before your death, you will remain a prostitute after your death and if you did not undergo change, you will be reincarnated as a prostitute.

For you to change, you have to change the thought of what you are in your mind but an embody thought is difficult to change. For you to achieve this change, you have to continuously exert effort in thinking the thought of what you want to be which will displace the thought of what you are that will make change to be possible for you. The thought of what or who you are always resist change because your mind have taken the mold of what or who you are which your life have taken it form which make change to be extremely difficult but not impossible.

Your mind is comfortable with the type of you that you are because the type of person that you are make your gene to undergo mutation and change your body to the type of you that you are and the body make the mind to resist change because the body and the mind have influence on each other.

If you continue to exert effort to become the type of person that you want to be, your mind will influence your gene to undergo mutation to change your body and your body and your mind will change to the mold of the type of person that you want to be.

LIFE AFTER DEATH

People have different view concerning life after death. If you don't believe in life after death, continue to live a good life and do not preach against life after death so that you will not have much to lose if life after death is real. Let us assume that if there is life after death and you live a good life, when you die you will not have anything to lose but if there is life after death and you live a bad life, you will have everything to lose.

The state of death is the state of changing the body form and Apostle Paul confirm this in 1 Corinthians chapter 15 verse 51 that we shall not all fall asleep in death but be changed.

First Peter chapter 3, verse 19 to 20 say that Jesus went to preach to the spirit in prison that were disobedient in the days of Noah when the patient of God was waiting while the ark was being constructed in which only eight people were carried safely through the water. This is talking about dead people that were put in prison for their disobedient.

In the transfiguration of Jesus, Moses and Elijah appear one at the right hand side of Jesus and the other at the left hand side. If there is no life after death, where did Moses and Elijah appear from since both of them have died long before the transfiguration?

If anyone want to use suicide as a means of escape from a difficult problem, the state of death is not the end of any person's life. The one that commit suicide will create more problem for himself or herself with the suicide act.

If anyone have a serious problem, all problems have an expiry date if the problem seem to defy solution. Every problem is telling us that we are deficient in living in accord with the law that govern life and that we need correction to start living in accord with the law that govern life. It is ignorant of the law that make many people to break the law and ignorant of the law is not an excuse for breaking the law for anyone that break the law whether knowingly or unknowingly will be punish by the law.

If anyone use suicide to escape from a difficult problem, such one will be judge guilty by the judge of the dead for taking his or her own life and will be reincarnated to face the problem that he or she is running away from all over again because everyone must pay his or her moral and spiritual debt.

Every problem have the lesson that is bring and if you refuse to learn the lesson that a problem bring, the problem will keep repeating itself until you learn the lesson that it bring.

Every problem is meant for the maturity of every person that the problem concern. Everyone should meet every problem with the mind of solving the problem and not to run away from the problem because any problem you run away from will be waiting for you.

I hear in the news some time ago about a man that commit suicide because the football team that this man was a fan of was beaten by another football team. A lot of reporters give different comment about the man in relation with the football tournament. When I hear it in the news, I know that a big problem must have been going on in his mind that seem to defy solution prior to the time of the football tournament. Many people think that the man committed suicide because of the loss of the game by the football team which he is a fan of but this is not the case. The man must have been nursing the thought of suicide in his mind for some time before the team which he is a fan of lost the game that make him to commit suicide. The lost of the game make him to be courageous enough to commit suicide because it was the lost of the game that gave him the courage to commit suicide.

There are different type of extreme difficult problem that can make a sane person to think of committing suicide and if the thought is accepted it can lead to committing suicide. Suicide cannot solve any problem, it will add to the problem. Death should not be an option even if the extreme problem defy solution. Any problem that we cannot solve we will be adapted to with the passing of time if it defy solution.

It is only those that are living a good life that death will be a good thing to because their death will be the passage to heaven but for those that are living a bad life, death will be a bad thing to them because their death will be a passage to hell. To those living a bad life, it is better for them to live than to die and it is better for one to live than to commit suicide.

Sometime thinking of killing oneself can be a hypnotic effect from someone that is hypnotizing you to kill yourself and the hypnotic effect will affect you if you accept it.

It is the mind that analyze problem and see one to be big and the other to be small and the mind exaggerate some problem giving them a different meaning.

If you have any problem that seem to defy solution, with the passing of time, your mind will become calm to the problem, and you will see the way to solve the problem.

The only reason anyone that harbor the thought of suicide have not commit suicide is because of the fear of the pain of death and if anything can make anyone that harbor the thought of suicide to overcome fear, the person will end up committing suicide.

Problem are meant for the maturity of everyone and the more problems you solve, the more experience you will have and the more matured you will be. As everything have an expiry date, so every problem, no matter how hard it may be have an expiry date. As day pass after day, so the problem will reduce if you did not do anything that add to it.

There are four schools of thought concerning life after death. The first school of thought state that when you die, you will pass through judgement and if judgement is in favor of you, you will go to heaven and if judgement is against you, you will go to hell. Some assume hell to be a place of burning lake of fire where disobedient soul will burn forever while some assume hell to be a place of eternal destruction that will make a soul to cease to exist. Whichever you believe in, hell is not a place that anyone should wish to see.

The second school of thought state that when you die, you will cease to exist to be resurrected to face judgement, if judgement is in your favor, you will live eternally and if judgement is against your favor, you will be destroyed.

The third school of thought state that this world is the middle of creation where good and evil exist side by side and when a good person die, the good person will die to the level of the higher world that match the level of the person's good and continue development and keep ascending according to the rate of the person's development if the person did not have atonement that will bring the person back to this world. When an evil person die, the evil person will die to the lower world that match the level of the person's evil and ascend if the person develop to good or descend if the person develop to evil. If a good person keep ascending to good, the person will become good up to the level that the person will ascend to paradise, an eternal bliss. When an evil person keep descending to evil, the evil person will descend to the level of evil that will make the evil person meet eternal destruction, the type of destruction that the Bible called a second death, a type of death that will make the soul cease to exist. The planet earth and it solar system is the middle point because it is the point where good and evil dwell side by side and outside the planet earth, good have it place and evil have it place and they don't have any form of contact. It is like the illustrative story of Lazarus and the rich man that after their death, two of them have no form of contact and cannot because one is good and the other is evil. Like the educational system that we get promoted to a higher class when our educational level is above the class that we are in so we get promoted to the next higher world after our maturity have grown beyond the level of the maturity of the world we are in and if we continue in the progress of maturity we will become perfect and gain entry to paradise the perfect city where everything is perfection. Christianity believe that paradise, the abode of the blessed is the highest world but another religion sect believe that there is always one world ahead. Apostle Paul said in 2 Corinthians chapter 12 verse 2 to verse 4 that he saw a man in union with Christ that was able to peep to the third heaven and to paradise. If there is a third heaven, according to the Bible, then there must be a first and a second heaven which confirm that there are worlds outside this our planet earth world. This world, the planet earth is a place where every calibre of being dwell side by side including the powerful being that we cannot see with our physical eyes. When any being leave this world, the being cannot go beyond the world that is beyond the level of the being maturity. The being will become unconscious if a higher being take a lower mature being there because the pressure there will make the lower being unconscious. This is similar to the educational system where you take someone of a lower educational level to a higher educational level, the person will not understand what they teach there because the educational standard of the person is not up to the level. The highest height is a state of perpetual bliss and any soul that can ascend there is back home to God. The deepest depth is a state of nothing and any soul that descends there will become nothing and this will be an eternal death for the soul.

The fourth school of thought state that when a person die, all have ended for the person, the person will cease to exist. This school of thought is base on the fact that life after death cannot be investigated with any scientific equipment and people that investigate life after death through occult practice could not rationally prove it.

The people that believe in life after death could not rationally prove it and various religion books that speak on life after death did not have proof to back them up and there is no one that can prove them. People that did not believe in life after death and say that there is no life after death cannot prove that when a person die, the person will cease to exist. What every person need to do is to live a good life so that if life after death is real, one will not have anything to lose when the person face the reality and if there is no life after death, one will also not have anything to lose. But because no one can rationally prove a thing did not mean that the thing did not exist.

Live a good life till your dying day and when you die, you will know whether life after death exist or not because if you live a good life you will not have anything to lose but if you live a bad life, you will have everything to lose.

If anyone die and come back to life to say that there is life after death, many people will consider it to be a lie and death is not a journey that anyone can go and come back to tell the story.

Some people assume death to be similar to dream, some assume death to be a wakeless sleep while some assume death to be a state of change in consciousness. Whichever you assume to be true is base on your level of understanding of life and death. Everyone are entitle to their opinion and no one have the right to condemn the opinion of another person if the opinion is not hostile to life and since everyone will die one day, everyone will face the reality.

REINCARNATION

10

John the Baptist is Elijah that is destine to come, he who have ears let him hear – Jesus

ARGUMENT OVER REINCARNATION

Reincarnation is an issue that many people are for or against all over the world. Everyone are entitle to their opinion but a wrong opinion cannot become right and change reality if everyone believe in it.

If anyone don't want to believe in reincarnation, let the person not preach against reincarnation and live a good life and such one will not have business with reincarnation.

The reason for reincarnation is to come to another earth life to atone for the wrong one have done to the world and the wrong one have done to another person and become free of the debt of the wrong. If anyone is owing any form of debt, the person is not a free person until the person pay the debt.

It is materialism that propel one to do the wrong that bind one to the world and it is hate and emotional love that propel one to do the wrong that bind one to another person. Any form of binding make the person binded to be a slave of the bond and until the person become free of the bond through atonement, the person will remain a slave of the bond.

Emotional love and hate are powerful emotion that bind two people together and if one is reincarnated, the other will also be reincarnated. If you hate another person or you love someone emotionally, you are binding yourself to the person and if the person is reincarnated, you will also be reincarnated along with the person.

If you are ascending to the world of light and you hate or you emotionally love another person, the person you hate or emotionally love will serve as a downward pull on you and prevent your ascent.

For anyone to be free from reincarnation, such one must not live his or her life to influence people to evil and such one must not do anything to bring out evil in another person. For instance, if you are rich, you must not influence anyone to lust, you must not parade your wealth to make anyone jealous and you must not display your wealth to make the poor look down on themselves. These are some of the reason Jesus said that it will be difficult for a rich person to enter the kingdom of God because many rich people unconsciously do these things.

Some people did not believe in reincarnation reasoning that if reincarnated is true, there is no justice in reincarnation if someone is reincarnated without knowing the reason for the reincarnation. Everybody intuitive know what is right and what is wrong but many people choose to ignore their intuition and nature have no time to explain to anyone what everyone know through their intuition which is the God given indwelling ability in everyone to know right from wrong.

If everybody know the reason they are reincarnated, they will refuse to live their life to the fullest and watch life pass them bye instead of to live and learn the lesson of life.

For those that did not believe in reincarnation but believe in a judgement day, can a petty thief that steal to satisfy his or her need and an armed thief that steal to satisfy his or her greed be destroy for the same reason? And if you believe in hell fire, will a petty thief and an armed thief burn in the same hell fire? Will a petty thief that steal something petty and a armed thief that steal with the aim to kill anyone that obstruct him or her burn in the same burning hell fire in the same degree or in a different degree?

A petty thief will be reincarnated to atone for his or her petty stealing and the armed thief will be reincarnated to atone for his or her armed stealing. A petty thief steal due to his or her laziness and the armed thief steal due to his or her greed. Since the petty thief and the armed thief are thieves of different level, they cannot pass through the same punishment but are to be reincarnated and atone for stealing due to laziness and stealing due to greed.

BIBLE REFERENCE TO REINCARNATION

In Malachi chapter 4 verse 5, it say, "I am sending to you Prophet Elijah before the great and dreadful day of the Lord arrive. His preaching will turn the heart of parents to their children and the heart of children to their parent. Otherwise, I will come and strike the land with a curse". This foretell the reincarnation of Prophet Elijah.

Matthew chapter 11 verse 13 to verse 14 say "For all the prophets and the law prophesied until John and if you want to accept it, he is Elijah that was destine to come, he who have ears, let him hear". This was Jesus speaking according to the record of Matthew. Jesus stated here that John the Baptist is the reincarnation of Elijah and it is not by force that anyone should accept it because reincarnation is beyond the understanding of many people.

Mark chapter 9 verse 11 – 13 support the record of Matthew by saying that they began to question Jesus asking "why did the scribes say that Elijah must come first" and Jesus said to them, "Elijah will come first and restore all things but as it is written about the son of man that he will go through many suffering and be treated of as nothing. But I say to you that Elijah have come and they did to him many things they wanted as it is written regarding him".

Those that say that there is no reincarnation supported their statement from what recorded in Luke chapter 1 verse 17 which say that John the Baptist will go before him with the spirit and power of Elijah to turn back the hearts of fathers to children and the disobedient ones to get ready for God a prepared people. With this verse, they say that John the Baptist is not the reincarnation of Elijah and that John the Baptist came with the same spirit and power as Elijah.

In Judaism, there are different sect and the prominent among the different sect are the Pharisee and the Sadducee. The Pharisee believe in life after death, reincarnation, and the existence of spirit but the Sadducee did not believe in any of these.

Luke is a Sadducee which influence his account of the synoptic gospel and record things that are more different from the gospel according to Matthew and Mark. Apostle Paul on the other hand was a Pharisee which make him to accept the teachings of Christ without any difficulty and did the greatest work for Christ base on his level of knowledge.

Luke rewrite the statement of Malachi in Malachi chapter 4 verse 5 that John the Baptist came with the same spirit and power as Elijah.

Matthew gave account that all the prophets and the law prophesied until John and that John is the reincarnation of Elijah but Luke gave the same report that all the Prophets and the Law were until John but omit the statement that John the Baptist is the reincarnation of Elijah.

Those that say there is no reincarnation also support themselves with the record of John chapter 1 verse 19 to verse 21 which say that this is the witness of John when the Jews sent forth priests and Levites from Jerusalem to ask him "who are you?". And he confessed and did not deny but confessed, "I am not Christ" and they ask him "are you Elijah?" and he said "no".

John the Baptist did not know that he is the reincarnation of Elijah, as you and I did not know about our previous life. Everyone are blindfolded from their past life so that it should not have effect on their present life. For instance, in your previous life, if you are a wicked spouse and in this life your spouse is to be wicked to you as the atonement for being wicked to your spouse. Knowing this, you may refuse to marry knowing that anyone that you marry will be wicked to you as the payment of the wrong you did to your spouse in your past life.

Jesus said that the least person in the kingdom of God is greater than John the Baptist which mean that the ability of John the Baptist to endure is limited. If John the Baptist know that he will be beheaded by Herod as the atonement for the slaughter of the prophet of Baal, he would not have warn Herod against the marriage of his brother's wife that lead Herod to beheaded him, he will have simply keep quiet rather than to endure being beheaded by Herod as Jesus Christ endure Judas as one of his twelve disciples and later betray Jesus to death on the cross.

John chapter 3 verse 31 say that Jesus said "he that come from above is above all others, he that is from the earth speak things of the earth".

If Jesus that is from above say that John the Baptist is the reincarnation of Elijah as stated in Matthew chapter 11 verse 13 and Mark chapter 9 verse 11 to verse 13, should we earth men assume that John the Baptist is not the reincarnation of Elijah even if John the Baptist is not aware that he is the reincarnation of Elijah.

Jesus know that some things are difficult to understand which always make him to end his saying by saying that let him that have ears to hear hear and it also make him to speak in illustration.
It was stated in John chapter 3 verse 12 that Jesus said, "if I tell you earthly things and you did not believe, how will you believe if I tell you heavenly things". With this statement, it shows that there are earthly things and there are heavenly things that are difficult to believe.

Luke that says that John the Baptist came with the spirit and power as Elijah is not among the twelve disciples of Jesus therefore, he did not hear Jesus say so. He hear it from another person because he did not say that Jesus said that John the Baptist is not the reincarnation of Prophet Elijah. The record of Luke is base on what was handed to him and a first hand story is not like the second and a third hand story. If Matthew and Mark that were among the twelve disciples of Jesus say that Jesus said that John the Baptist is Elijah that was destine to come and Malachi said that Elijah came as John the Baptist, do we have to leave these three people that one is a prophet and the other two are among the twelve disciples that receive teaching from Jesus and believe the statement of Luke that is not a prophet nor was he among the twelve disciples that receive teachings directly from Jesus?

Elijah was reincarnated as John the Baptist to prepare the way for the coming of Christ and also to atone for the slaughter of the prophet of Ball to be beheaded by Herod.
One may argue that Elijah was doing the work of God by slaughtering the prophet of Baal but killing is killing whether it is for God or for any other reason. Any person that kill in the name of God will atone for the killing in the name of God. Unchangeable is the law that governs life.
Jesus said that with the measure that you measure out will be measured back to you. Elijah kill but he was too powerful to be killed, he did not taste death but ascend to heaven – 2 King chapter 2 verse 11. Since he was too powerful to be killed, he reincarnated as meek John the Baptist to prepare the way of Christ and also to be beheaded as the atonement for slaughtering the prophet of Baal.

As powerful as Elijah is, for he ascended to heaven without tasting death, Jesus said that the least person in the kingdom of God is greater than John the Baptist. This mean that Elijah did not ascend to paradise the perfect city of God, he ascend to one of the heaven stated by Apostle Paul in 2 Corinthians chapter 12.
There are many things that are difficult to understand and Jesus state it when he said "If I tell you earthly things and you did not believe, how will you believe if I tell you heavenly things".

THE
SECRET
OF THE
CONCEPTION
OF
CHRIST

11

The Holy Spirit will come upon Mary and the power of the most high will overshadow Mary and she will become pregnant – Angel Gabriel

THE POSSIBILITY

Many people think that it is impossible for Mary, the mother of Jesus to become pregnant with the pregnancy of Jesus without having any union with a man.

If you are ignorant of a knowledge in a particular field, except you are shown the secret of the knowledge, it will be difficult to believe the reality of the knowledge especially if it is hard to understand.

Consider this, if people in the days of Jesus were told that at this our present time, someone in Jerusalem will be able to speak with another person in London and see each other's face to face as if they were talking to each other face to face. The person saying this may be considered insane because the level of the technological development in the days of Jesus was in the kinder garden level compare to this our modern technological development which will be beyond the understanding of the people of the days of Jesus. If another person in the days of Jesus say that a type of vehicle will be able to fly in this our modern era, they will consider the person to be the greatest liar.

A human cell has 46 chromosomes and each chromosome has a DNA (deoxyribonucleic acid) that regulate the activity of each chromosome. A gene in each chromosome contains the genetic material in a coded form and a RNA (ribonucleic acid) that decode the genetic information in the gene according to the regulation of the DNA. Out of the 46 chromosome in the human cell, the gene of one chromosome has the coded information about the formation of the leg, another gene of another chromosome has the coded information about the formation of the hand. The gene in each chromosome of the 46 chromosome has different coded information about the formation of different part of the body.

The gonad which is the ovary in the female and the testes in the male split the human cell which is of 46 chromosomes into two which is a half cell with 23 chromosomes each which mean that a female ovary release an egg cell with 23 chromosomes and the male testes release a sperm cell with 23 chromosomes each. At conception, the 23 chromosomes of the egg cell of the female unite with the 23 chromosomes of the sperm cell and form the complete human cell of 46 chromosomes with half of the gene from the female and the other half from the male.

One of the 23 chromosomes of the female and one of the 23 chromosomes of the male are sex chromosomes because they determine the sex of the child whether the child will be a boy child or a girl child. This one sex chromosome in the female have a double X alleles, that is XX alleles and this one sex chromosome in the male have a XY alleles. If one X allele from the female unite with the X allele from the male, the child will be a girl child and if the other X allele from the female unite with the Y allele from the male, the child will be a boy child.

Before Mary become pregnant by the Holy Spirit with the pregnancy that form the body of Jesus, the Bible say that the Holy Spirit descend upon Mary and overshadow her and she become pregnant. When the Holy Spirit descend, it descend in the form of radiation, for example, as it happen in the day of Pentecost when the Holy Spirit descend on one hundred and twenty people in the form of a tongue of fire. It is this same form of radiation that radiate on Mary and cause the ovary of Mary not to split the egg that form the body of Jesus and release a complete cell of 46 chromosomes that did not need fertilization because it is half cell of 23 chromosomes that need another half cell of 23 chromosomes to fertilize it and make it a complete human cell of 46 chromosomes that grow the human body. With this the birth of Jesus was suppose to be a girl child since Mary being a female did not have a Y allele in her chromosome that is responsible for the formation of a male body. What happen was that the radiation that radiate on Mary that cause the gonad of Mary to release a complete cell of 46 chromosomes that did not need fertilization also cause the egg cell that form the body of Jesus to undergo mutation by changing it genetic code to make it form a male body.

Scientist are aware that radiation can make a cell to undergo mutation by changing if genetic code and example of it is a cancer cell which is expose to a type of radiation that change it genetic code.

WHO IS JESUS?

People see Jesus from different perspective. Some see him as a great prophet, some see him as the son of God and some see him as God. Everyone must remember that whatever his or her opinion is did not earn him or her the right to condemn the opinion of another person if the opinion is not hostile to life.

A moth have the opinion that fire is a play thing and it keep playing with fire and fire keep burning the moth to death and no one have the right to condemn the moth for playing with fire. If everyone condemned the moth, there is nothing anyone can do about it.

Christ is a special being and since he is a special being, he needs a special body for his spirit to dwell. A body that don't have to come to life through sex but through purity that is without sex which have to come to life through the virgin Mary because of the spiritual power that is of Christ.

To confirm that Jesus is the Christ, the bringer of truth to mankind, a truth that will lead everyone to salvation if they live by the truth of Christ. Let us look at the world calendar system. There are different calendar system in the world and many of them are base on the circle of the moon but it is the calendar system that is base on the birth of Jesus that is worldly accepted even though the whole world did not believe in Jesus. Although the calendar system of the world have it own story but it could have been rejected if it is not base on the uniqueness of Jesus.

The world start to count down from an archaic date down to the day Jesus was born and start to count up after the day Jesus was born up to this our present moment and beyond it. Some may say that it is a coincidence but is it a coincidence for the world to start to count down from an archaic date down to the day Jesus was born and start to count upward from then? Some say that the day Jesus was born is an assumption but there is no one that can prove with evidence that it is an assumption. Everyone are speculating because the date coincide with the day of the celebration of the sun god. Whether the date is a fact or not, since the light which is the positive is in everyone and Christ is the light of God that is in everyone, everyone accepted the day Jesus Christ was born unconsciously which make the world to start counting the new calendar system after his birth from the old calendar system that end with his birth.

It is claim by a religion sect that Jesus Christ is the reincarnation of Krshna, the holy one of the Hindus although many fantasy are created on the lifetime of Krshna.

There is no difference in the strict teaching of Krshna and the strict teaching of Jesus Christ. The Bhagavad gita say that Krshna is the beginning of all causes and the Bible state that Christ is the beginning of creation.

THE DEATH OF CHRIST

Jesus Christ could not have die on the cross, he could have ascend to heaven without tasting death as Prophet Elijah ascend to heaven without tasting death in his time as Elijah. Jesus die a painful death on the cross due to the sins of the people that he took upon himself and heal them. The blind was able to see because he took their sin upon himself, so is the lame that walk and the dead that he raise which warrant Jesus to die a painful death on the cross as the atonement of the sin of the people he took upon himself.

Jesus said that the heaven and the earth will pass away but one letter of the law will not pass without it fulfillment and the law state that everyone will reap what they sow.

It is sin that bring pain, poverty, disaster, and death and before any healing can be permanent, the cause which is the sin must be taken away through atonement.

Jesus die a horrible death on the cross as the atonement of the sin of the people he took upon himself. Nothing is free and anything that appear to be free have been paid for by another person whether we are aware of it or not.
Have you ever consider how painful it is to be nailed to a cross under the heat of the sun and die slowly until death? Do you think that the good God desire this for Jesus so that Jesus can be a sacrificial lamb for the forgiveness of the sin of the people that believe him, even the harden criminal that kill without mercy. If you think that God use Jesus as the sacrifice for the forgiveness of sin of many people, who did God sacrifice the sacrifice to? Is it to Himself or to another being? If God use Jesus as a sacrifice to Himself, then God is blood tasty God and if God use Jesus as sacrifice to another being, I cannot follow a God that use human for sacrifice which make the story of Jesus being use as a sacrifice for the forgiveness of the sin of many to be a fiction.

CHRIST AND RELIGION

Religion belief is an intellectual opinion, within the mind of everyone and deeply rooted either a positive characteristic or a negative one which form the individual behavior that define our hidden belief and it is this belief that mould our life and not the intellectual opinion that we call religion.

Jesus did not bring a new religion. What Jesus brought was a way of life that will lead people to God. Christianity that is name after Jesus is not a religion, it is movement of people that Jesus organize to spread the good news that will lead people to God and they were name Christian in Antioch which mean the likeness of Christ.
Anyone that practice Christianity as a religion is not practicing Christianity, the person is practicing Judaism which Jesus came from. Jesus supported Judaism although did not live by all the law of Judaism, for example the law of sabbath, the law of eating and many other doctrine of Judaism. Jesus did not condemn Judaism nor did he condemn any other religion, what Jesus demand from everyone is for everybody to live a good life, a life that will lead one to God.

Christ is the personification of the word of God and anywhere the word of God is being preach, they are preaching Christ, they are therefore Christian.
The Muslim are Christians because they preach the word of God and beside this, the name of Jesus appear so many times in the Quran, they are for Jesus therefore they are Christian.
Jesus said that he that is not against him is for him, any person that is not against Jesus is for Jesus. If we follow the history of the Muslim, they are the descendant of Abraham but not of the slave girl, the maid of Sarah as many assume. When Rebekah, The wife of Isaac was pregnant with the pregnancy of the twins Esau and Jacob, they inquire from God about the pregnancy and God said that there are two Nation in the womb of Rebekah. The two nations are the descendant of Esau and Jacob. God have already bless Ishmeal to be a great

nation and Esau went to Ishmeal to take his daughter Mahalath as a wife – Genesis chapter 28 verse 9. Since Ishmeal was with a great promise and Esau and Jacob are with a great promises when Esau and Mahalath unite in marriage, The promise of Ishmeal pass through his daughter Mahalath and unite with the promise of Esau with their generation that came up with the Muslim religion.
If you follow the history of Muslim religion, it is Angel Gabriel, a messenger of God that speaks the holy Quran to Mohammed Therefore the Holy Quran is a scripture from God.

Christ is the way, the truth and the life, therefore any religion that is not against the truth is for the truth. Every religion that preach the way of God and the truth of God are preaching Christ, the word of God that lead to life which is the mission of Jesus to show everyone the way that lead to life and are Christian because they follow the teaching of Christ.
Remember that Christianity is not a religion, it is the way that lead to life, but the follower of Christ later deviate from the teaching of Christ – Revelation chapter 2 verse 4 and organize a religion base on the doctrine of Judaism.
The disciples of Jesus use to worship at the temple but due to the persecution against them, they left worshipping at the temple and turn Christianity to a religion which was not the aim of Jesus because Jesus said in Matthew chapter 5 verse 17 that he did not come to destroy Judaism but the follower of Christ destroy Judaism by using Judaism to create Christianity, a new religion that is not the intention of Jesus.
Christianity was suppose to be a movement of people from different religion that follow the teachings of Jesus and to help to spread the gospel of truth to their various religion that will make the world a peaceful place for everyone to live

When there is diversity and there is no nucleus to unite the diversity then there will be chaos. The mission of Jesus is to unite the diversity and bring every religion to God.
Jesus said that he had other sheep which are not of the Christian fold that listen to his voice and he will bring them and they will become one flock, one shepherd – John chapter 10 verse 16.This fold that Jesus was talking about are of different religion and Jesus was saying here that he will bring every religion together and they will become one flock of one shepherd.
If the world in their different religion claim to worship God and could not unite in their different ways of worshipping the same God, there can never be peace in the world until the world start to accept each other in their diversity as the norm of life after all every person are not of the same color which is a prove that God created diversity in life.

The follower of Christ deviate from the mission of Christ which is to bring every religion to God. It is Apostle Paul that is a true Christian, a true follower of Christ that lives by the mission of Christ.

Apostle Paul is a Jew to the Jews and when he is with the Romans, he behave like a Roman in order to win the heart of Romans. He is under the law to those under the law (Judaism) and he is not under the law to those not under the law (Gentiles).
Apostle Paul is a nucleus that unites every diversity to Christ and this is what a true Christian should be and this make him different from the other Apostles. Other Apostle consider Paul to be fanatic but it is they that are fanatic because they misunderstand the mission of Christ as a nucleus that unite diversity. Christianity should extract itself from Judaism and be the nucleus that lead people to God and not a nucleus that generate diversity by saying that salvation belong to Christianity.

From Jacob came the Christian and from Esau came the Muslim, the two major religion that dominate the world.
Christianity and Islam are brothers and they are suppose to be in accord even though they have their differences. Everywhere they are good people and bad people. A people are said to be good people if the percentage of the good people is more than the percentage of the bad people and a people are said to be bad people if the percentage of the bad people is more than the percentage of the good people.

The sin of one is the sin of all and the virtue of one is the virtue of all. Let me explain this. If one person sin, the sin will have effect on the world and the effect of the sin of the world will have effect on everyone in the world because everyone is part of the world.
The effect of the sinner is on the world and the effect of the world is on us thereby bringing disorder to the world which extends to everyone in the world. The effect of a saint is on the world which have effect on us. A saint bring peace and order to the world and the peace and order extend to everyone in the world while a sinner bring war and disorder to the world which extend to everyone in the world.

If your religion can produce saint to the world, whether I am in agreement with your religion or not, I will benefit from the saintly life of the saint that your religion produce. But if I condemn your religion and your religion stop producing saint and become sinner, the effect of it will be upon everyone. Let us learn to tolerate each other's religion if the religion is not hostile to life.

Let us change the world by changing ourselves first and if we change ourselves, we will become an example to the other person to change.
You cannot change me by condemning me. If we condemn each other we will end up creating distance between each other which will create an environment that is hard for change.

THE VIRUS THAT CRACK THE WORLD

According to the Bible, death came to life through one man which make the sin of one to be the sin of all.
From time to time, virus that cause destruction to human have been coming to life to torment human due to human sin, but how are these virus coming to life?

A virus have no life of its own, it is only a coiled nucleic acid in a protein coat and it exist in nature in the form of a crystal. Crystal is a clear quartz like ice and when it is a virus, it is a virus that is a coiled nucleic acid embedded in a protein coat in the form of a crystal.
A virus is the transition from the non to the non living which make it have a dual state. It can only exist in a living state inside a cell by using the DNA of a cell to give itself life and reproduce itself and outside a cell it exist in a crystal form.

A virus is deadly because inside a cell, it use the DNA of a cell for it own genetic programme thereby making the cell die for it to become living using the life of a cell for it own life.
The virus in it non living state is harmless to a cell and it is only harmful when something power the non living virus to make use of the DNA of a cell to give itself life and become destructive by using the DNA of a cell for itself to become alive.

God command that no one should touch a dead animal and anyone that touch a dead animal should remain unclean for a period of time and until the period of time complete, the person should not make contact with anyone and if the person by chance make contact with anyone, the person contacted should also remain unclean and until a cleansing ritual is made, they should not come to the society.
Thunder can power a virus crystal to use the DNA of an animal cell to become alive and reproduce itself thereby killing the animal. When human touch this dead animal, the virus will enter the person using the DNA of the cell of the person to reproduce which will make the person to transfer the virus among human race. It is this that make God to command human not to touch a dead animal and anyone that touch a dead animal should remain in isolation for a period of time.

God command human not to interbreed animal but the interbreeding of the genome of different animals in order to produce new effective drug is what take place in the laboratory of genetic engineering.
In the process of interbreeding the genome of an animal cells, they can mistakenly give power to a crystal virus that find it way to the lab to use the DNA of a cell in their lab to come to life and start hunting the DNA of human cells. The solution to this is for genetic engineer to quarantine themselves after a genetic interbreeding.

The sin of one is the sin of all. A sin of one religion have effect on another religion whether the religion realize it or not because the coronavirus that originate from a part of the world that have it own religion is having effect on every other religion because the coronavirus is shutting down people coming together which prevent the coming together of every religion to worship their God because of the fear of contacting coronavirus.

If every religion can become their brother's keeper and therefore aid the other to produce many saint to the world rather than to condemn the other, every dangerous disease will not come to life because the light of God that dwell in saint will prevent every dangerous disease that will threaten the life of everyone to come to life because there is no form of darkness no matter how powerful it is can come near the light.

The river have overflowing it boundary in West Africa causing destruction of lives and properties. All over the world, one catastrophe or the other have been threatening human life from year to year and the greatest of all is the deadly coronavirus that shut down more than half of the world. Is this the end of the world? But definitely, this is not the end of the world because Jesus said that there is no one that knows the end of the world except God the creator of life.

We human can put an end to all these catastrophe by living according to the law of God which is an unconditional love. Let all the religions of the world love themselves unconditionally without looking to the petty fault of each other. We are all the creature of God and let us all live according to the will of God and all these global epidemic will cease.

Coronavirus is an example to the world that our knowledge, our wisdom and our understanding of nature cannot save us from the punishment by nature. We human are wise only to ourselves and God said that he will catch us in our wisdom and a holy book said that our wisdom is foolishness before God. Let us all summit to the will of God and many ill in our life will be corrected.

Jesus Christ state that the laws of God are only in two parts. The first part is to love God will all our mind, all our soul, and all our strength and the second is to love our neighbor as ourselves. The question now is who is our neighbor? Our neighbor is the person next to us whether in our front or in our back or in our two side. Our neighbor is the next religion to us whether from the west, the east, the south or the north.

The next person to me is my neighbor and the next person to my neighbor is the neighbor of my neighbor and the next person to the neighbor of my neighbor is the neighbor of the neighbor of my neighbor which make everyone to be neighbor. If we are to love God with all our mind and all our strength, we must love our neighbor as ourselves because we cannot love god without loving our neighbor.

THE RELIGION OF LOVE

Apostle Paul said that faith, hope, and love, love is the greatest of all. He further said that if anyone have faith that can move mountain and the person have no love, the person is nothing.

A popular Nigerian artist, Asa, gave me a lot of inspiration through her music from her old song up to this moment. One of her song from her hit album, "fire on the mountain" is a song that always give me inspiration anytime I hear it. The lyric of the song say that there is fire on the mountain and no one is on the run. According to the song, no one seem to care if there is fire on the mountain. The song went further to say that tomorrow is the day that Mr. Soldier Man will go to war and it was asking the soldier the reason for going to the war whether the soldier is going to war because of the love for his country or because of the love of the gun the soldier use in killing. This remind me of a young man I met in a village some time ago. A militant group came to the town with a sophisticated gun, a model of gun I have not seen except in the hand of soldier in a deadly hot zone. The young man was so entice to the sight of the gun that he express his love for the gun. If this young man happen to join the military force, the young man will go to war because of the love of the gun the young man will use in killing and not the love the young man have for his country. According to Asa, going to war is to settle another man's score and victory is not even sure which I agree with.

Asa spread the gospel of love with her music demanding everyone to love one another, whoever a person is, is to love whoever another person is. I am walking in the same footprint with Asa with my book spreading the gospel of love through inspirational writing demanding every nation, every religion, and every people to love one another.

Asa said in her music that one day the water will overflow and there will be nowhere for us to go if we neglect to live with her gospel of love. Now the water have overflow with coronavirus and there is nowhere we can run to, to escape coronavirus. If we keep neglecting to live by the religion of love, the water will keep overflowing up to the point that it will drown the world.

PUBLIC INFORMATION ON THE DREADED

CORONAVIRUS AND PREVENTIVE MEASURES-

The book did not have ISBN because of the temporary close down of the national library due to coronavirus epidemic.
When the office reopen, ISBN will be purchase for it.
Publish by Golden Ray Books
No. 12b, behind No. 12 Amame Street, Irri
Delta State.
09072671121, 08116297948

CONTENT

INTRODUCTION

I did not intend to write a small book like this but I compel myself to write it because of the deadly coronavirus that is threatening the existence of human life and be of a low price that will make many people to afford it.

I am a gifted writer and this is my first book to be publish and before writing this book, I have written and typeset a book "THE SECRET OF LIFE" that I could have publish if not for the deadly coronavirus that is shutting down many countries of the world. I have another book that is yet to be typesetted "THE SECRET OF MONEY". With the book, I want to use myself as an example that any person can rise from extreme poverty to riches because it is my extreme poverty that make me to study the life of the rich and the life of the poor and come up with a concrete proof that any poor person can become rich, no matter the level of poverty and use myself as the example for it.

There was a time that I was sick and look normal to people but inside me, I was sick. I went to the hospital and they could not find solution to my health problem and one of the hospital staff suggest that my illness is psychological. With the believe that it may be

psychological, I thought that the sickness was spiritual, so I start going from one herbalist (witchdoctor) to the other but there was no solution. I abandon going to herbalist and start going from one religion to the other which broaden my scope about God, religion, and the existence of life but I could not find the solution to my ailment.
In the course of my search for solution, I met a woman that introduce me to GNLD's nutritional supplement which gave me a partial solution. GNLD have the right supplement but many of GNLD practioner at a certain level did not have the knowledge of the symptom of deficiency and overdose.
I acquire the knowledge of deficiency and overdose from various source and I went into the study of human anatomy and nutrition in relation to excess and deficit of nutrition in relation to human health. And my deep knowledge gave birth to this book.

1

WHAT IS A VIRUS

A virus is not a cell, it is a coiled nucleic acid enclose in a protein coat. It is the border line between non living and living thing.
In a non living state, a virus exist in the form of a crystal and in the living state, it can only exist inside a cell by using the DNA of the cell for if genetic programme and use it to replicate itself thereby killing the cell to make itself a living thing inside the cell.

The transition of a virus from the non living state to a living state is powered by electrical energy from the thunder during a thunder storm when the virus come in contact with a cell.

2

THE ORIGIN OF CORONAVIRUS

The coronavirus come to life from the genetic engineering lab through the cross breeding of gene from different cells to produce powerful drugs to treat ailment.

A non living virus is harmless and it can drift about in nature not causing harm to anyone or anything.
The non living virus must have drift to the genetic engineering lab and powered by their genetic test to come alive through the cell that the engineer are using for their experiment.

3

THE EFFECT OF CORONAVIRUS

Every virus don't use the DNA of every cell to replicate itself, it target a cell that can match it nucleic acid to replicate itself. Coronavirus therefore use the DNA of the cilia of the trachea and the lower respiratory system to replicate itself, thereby obstructing their function to human health.

The function of the cilia of the trachea is to sweep dust and other debris that is trap by the mucosa of the trachea with mucus upward to the throat either to be swallowed to the stomach or expel through the mouth.
When the cilia get destroyed by coronavirus, the mucus along with dust and other debris accumulate in the trachea to the point that they will block the trachea and prevent air passage to the lungs which make the person to die of suffocation.

4

THE MEANS OF CONTACTING CORONAVIRUS

The coronavirus is a virus that is highly infectious but cannot withstand a hot or acidic environment which is why it is being killed by the stomach acid if it get to the stomach.
We can not contact it through sex because of the acidic nature of the vaginal. The only entrance of coronavirus is through the eyes, the nose, and the mouth that lead to the respiratory tract.

Coronavirus cannot spread easily in a hot environment but spread very easy in a cold environment which make it seem as if it is a rich man sickness.
Why it spread easy among the rich than the poor is that the rich cannot withstand the heat of the hot sun. In their house, air conditioner is everywhere, so is the office and the car. The only time they experience the hot sun is when they are moving from the office to the house or their transition from the car to any other building.
This did not mean that the poor are immune to coronavirus. There is nobody that is immune to coronavirus and any person will contact coronavirus if they come in contact with coronavirus.

The people that are most vulnerable to contact coronavirus are people with respiratory tract infection, people with weak immune system, smokers because smoking damage the cilia of the trachea, and old people because of their weak digestive system.

5
THE FALSE NEWS OF CORONAVIRUS

Some people stipulate that the Chinese want to become world power by using coronavirus to destroy America that is considered to be the present world power.
This rumour is very disgustive because coronavirus is killing people in China as well as in America and the Chinese cannot destroy themselves to become world power because a dead person cannot exercise power, it is only a living person that can exercise power.

Some Christian are assuming that the devil want to destroy the world with coronavirus and it is only those that carry the 666 mark on their forehead that will survive coronavirus. This rumour is absurd because there is no one that carry the mark of 666 on their forehead. The coronavirus is a living thing that exhibit the characteristic of a living thing which is to feed and reproduce itself and it have nothing to do with the devil.

Some people think that one extreme rich man in America want to initiate many people in Africa into a cult by donating relief material to them against coronavirus. This is an extremely bad rumour that is destroying the image of this rich man. A cult can only initiate a person that is useful to the cult and what can a poor Africans give to an extremely rich man cult.

Many local people raise a thought that a local concentrated alcohol called "ogogoro" can cure coronavirus by drinking it. An alcohol can kill coronavirus but to drink it cannot cure coronavirus because an alcohol pass through eosophagus to the stomach and not to the trachea where coronavirus is.

Some poor people are assuming that coronavirus is meant to destroy the rich as if the poor are immune to coronavirus. I met a poor man that was expressing happiness because he think that when the rich are destroyed, the wealth of the rich will belong to the poor. This poor person have a negative mindset and one thing this poor man fail to realize is that the poor cannot do without the rich just as the rich cannot do without the poor.

Some people think that chloroquine will cure coronavirus because chloroquine is part of the therapy against coronavirus. Chloroquine cannot cure coronavirus, it is use as an aid to the absorption of zinc to boost the immune system so that the immune system can fight coronavirus and overcome it.

Many substance that people think can cure coronavirus are not accepted by WHO because of their effect on the body system. There is no sane person that will accept the cure of a leg disease by destroying the hand and what is the essence of curing the leg to destroy the hand.

6

THE DEFENSE OF THE BODY AGAINST INFECTION

Some people inherit a nonspecific resistance to some infection which is called species resistance. This lie in the gene, when parent pass a gene of non specific resistance to their offspring that make the offspring immune to a particular viral or bacteria causing disease.

THE FIRST LINE OF DEFENSE

The first line of fight against virus, bacteria, or a pathogen is the epithelial tissue of the skin, mocouse membrane e.g the membrane (outer surface) of the digestive, respiratory, urinary, and reproductive tracts. These membrane may seem to be inside the body but they are outside the body because they are connected to the outside body. They serve as physical barriers and secrete a variety of protective chemicals.

Many people assume that taking a large dose of vitamin C can cure viral or bacteria infection but large dose of vitamin C have negative effect on the body. Indeed, it can cure infection only if the infection have not pass through the first line of defense which are the epithelial tissue because it is secreted in form of an acid that kill pathogens at the epithelial tissue.

The acid pH of the skin secretion inhibit bacteria growth e.g. sebum in particular contain chemicals that are toxic to bacteria and the vaginal secretion of an adult female are acidic.

The stomach mucosa secrete a concentrated hydrochloric acid solution and protein digesting enzymes both of which kill pathogens.

Saliva which cleanse the oral cavity (mouth) and teeth and lacrimal fluid which washes the external surface of the eyes contain lysozome, an enzyme that destroy bacteria.

Sticky mucus produce by the gastrointestinal and respiratory mucosa trap many microorganism that enter these passageway.

THE SECOND LINE OF DEFENSE

Although the surface barriers are effective but pathogens that make it through the first line of defense are confronted by a second line of defense.

Pathogens that escape the first line of defense infiltrate deeper tissue which make other non specific mechanism to come into fight to defend the body.

The body release macrophages, mast cells and some type of white blood cells and a dozen of chemical substances that contribute to pathogens killing and tissue repair. Antibacterial protein present in the blood or antiviral protein release by viral infected cells come into fight to defend the body.

Some bacteria such as bacillus that cause tuberculosis are resistance to digestion by macrophages. These bacteria are able to escape the effect of antibiotic by remaining snugly enclosed within their macrophage host in a granulomas capsule. A person may harbor pathogens walled off in a granulomas capsule for many years without displaying any symptoms of disease. If something happen to lower the person's resistance to infection, the encapsulated bacteria may become activated and breakout leading to symptom and the disease.

A virus infected cells can do little to save themselves, they help defend other cells by secreting small proteins called interferon. The interferon molecules diffuse to nearby cells and bind to their membrane receptors interfering with the ability of viruses to multiply within other cells.

Fever or abnormally high body temperature represent a systemic response to invading micro organisms.

Body temperature is regulated by a cluster of neurons in the hypothalamus, commonly referred to as body thermostat. The thermostat is reset upward in respond to chemicals called pyrogens which are secreted chiefly by macrophages exposed to bacteria and virus.

High fever are dangerous because of heat that inactivate enzymes. Mild or moderate fever benefit the body because large amount of iron proliferate but during the fever, the liver and spleen sequester iron making it less available. Fever also increase the metabolic rate of tissue cells speeding up defensive action and repair processes.

THE THIRD LINE OF DEFENSE

If the second line of defense cannot defend the body, then the third line of defense come up.

The body third line of defense is the immune system response.

It provide a unique protective service that is carefully targeted against specific antigens.

The immune system is a functional system that recognize antigens and acts to immobilize, neutralize, or destroy them.

When it operate effectively, the immune system protects the body from a wide variety infectious agents. When it fail, malfunction or disabled, devastating disease invade the body.

7

BUILDING THE LINE OF DEFENSE

BUILDING THE FIRST LINE OF DEFENSE

The first line of defense is the epithelial tissue (the outer surface of an organ system that lead outside the body), and to build it is to give it the nourishment that it need.

The nourishment of the first line of defense is vitamin A and vitamin C. But vitamin A cannot be absorb successfully without the aid of fatty food and fatty food cannot be digested without vitamin B_{12} and vitamin B_{12} cannot be absorb without intrinsic factor which make vitamin A to be the most deficient vitamin all over the world. And excess of vitamin C in the body lead to gout therefore it should be moderately taken. Fat have earn a bad reputation because many people don't want to be lumpy and many people avoid fat because of the health related problem that it generate but it can only generate health related problem when it is taken in excess. Too much of fat is bad for our health and too little of it is also bad to our health therefore moderation is the rule of the game. Oil that are plant fat can be use instead of animal fat because plant fat don't generate much problem as animal fat.

BUILDING THE SECOND LINE OF DEFENSE

The second line of defense depend on the strength of macrophages, mast cells, white blood cells, antiviral and antibacterial protein. The strength of these antibodies depend on vitamin B_5, B_6 and folic acid and the strength of white blood cells depends on copper.

BUILDING THE THIRD LINE OF DEFENSE

The third line of defense depend on the strength of the immune system.

The nourishment to build the immune system are vitamin A, vitamin E, iron and zinc.

8

THE BLOOD

It is the blood that take nutrient from the digestive system to the different organ of the body for their different use. So the power of the body to fight against disease depend on the strength of the blood to carry different nutrient to different part of the body for their use.

The body form blood in the red bone marrow or myeloid tissue found chiefly in the flat bones of the skull and pelvis, the ribs, sternum, and proximal epiphyses of the humerus and femur.

Leukocytes (white blood cells) is less numerous than erythrocytes (red blood cells) and they are crucial to the body defense against disease. They form a protective mobile army that protect the body from damage by bacteria, virus, parasite, toxins, and tumor cells. In the defense of the body, red blood cells are confined to the blood vessel and they carry out their function in the blood. White blood cells on the other hand are able to slip out of the blood vessel to where they mount immune response. Whenever white blood cells are mobilized for action, the body speed up their production and twice than normal may appear in the blood within a few hours.

The requirement to build blood in the bone marrow are protein, iron, folic acid, and vitamin B_{12}.

9

THE DIGESTIVE SYSTEM

The health of the body including the blood depend on the function of the digestive system and the absorption of food digested.

For digestion to function properly, the mucosa of the digestive tract must function properly and the functioning of the mucous membrane depend on vitamin A which make vitamin A to be important to the body and the proper functioning of all epithelial tissue in the body depend on vitamin A.

Digestion begin in the oral cavity (mouth). The digestion of carbohydrate begin in the oral cavity through an enzyme amylase from the saliva. Digestion of protein begin in the stomach through the stomach secretion of grastric acid and digestion of lipide (fat) take place in the duodenum through the bile salt.

The remaining food that is not digested is pass to the large intestine and decompose by the colon bacteria and pass out through the anus as feaces.

When digestion have taken place, the body have to absorb the food before the different organ of the body can make use of the digested food to repair damage tissue and synthesize chemicals to protect the body.

Vitamins and minerals supplement are already in their digested form there did not need digestion and are absorb immediately they are taken from the small intestine.

Absorption start from the stomach but the main site for absorption is the small intestine.

Some digested food cannot be absorb without the aid of another digested food. Fat soluble vitamin which are vitamin A, D, E, and K are fat soluble. It is fat that dilute them for them to pass through the absorption site and without fat, it is little of them that will be able to pass because of their viscosity (thickness). The other vitamins are water soluble. It is water that dilute them for them to pass through the absorption site except vitamin B_{12} that is fairly large that need intrinsic factor secreted by the stomach mucosa that aid it passage through the absorption site.

10

THE CIRCULATORY SYSTEM

When food are absorb through the small intestine into the arteries, blood carry the digested food round the body to cells of different organ to use it for energy, repair, and use it as an ammunition to defend the body against foreign invaders and abnormal body cells or criminal body cells.

Cell use the amino acid of protein to repair itself and to repair worn out cells, it use the starch of carbohydrate for energy, and it use fat of lipide to cushion the body and to protect adipose tissue. But cells cannot use protein, carbohydrate, or lipide without the aid of vitamins and minerals that propel their chemical reaction. If any vitamin or mineral is missing from the body, a part of the body will not function well because chemical reaction will not take place for it to function well. And to protect the body, cell use protein in combination with some vitamins and minerals to form it defensive army.

The blood is like a transport company that transport everything a cell need to it and transport the waste product a cell make away from the cell to the organ that dispose the waste away from the body.

The heart is like a pumping machine that pump blood round the body and it must function at a steady rate.

The heart must not be too fast which is high blood pressure but high blood pressure can also be caused by thinning of the blood. When the blood is too fast, nutrient and oxygen will not readily diffuse from the blood to the body cells because body cells take food supply from the blood through diffusion and food will not diffuse to them at the normal rate for them to function well.

The heart must not be slow which is low blood pressure but low blood pressure can also be caused by the viscosity of the blood. When the blood is slow, waste product that cells make will stay long in the body and become toxic to it.

The smooth working of the heart depend on intake of calcium and magnesium, the two minerals that are responsible for contraction and relaxation of all muscles of the body.

11

YOU ARE WHAT YOU EAT

The human cell contain 46 chromosomes and the gonad which are the testes and the ovary split the human cell which is of 46 chromosome into 23 chromosomes each.

At conception, the sperm cell which is of 23 chromosomes unite with the egg cell of the same 23 chromosomes to form the 46 chromosomes of the human cell.

The fertilize egg cell will continue to grow through cell division that will grow the different part of the body.

The cell will grow if the pregnant woman eat the different classes of food at their normal rate along with the appropriate vitamins and minerals. But if the pregnant woman neglect to eat a type of nutrition, a part of the body that depend on that nutrition for it function and growth will not develop well and it will become defective.

When the baby is born, the baby growth will depend on the nutrition from it mother's breast milk till the baby will be able to eat solid food.

When the baby start to eat solid food, the growth and proper function of the body depend on the type of food that the baby eat.

Children are not selective in what they eat, they eat what was given to them when they are hungry except an ill bred child that will command their parent on what to eat.

We adult on the other hand are selective on what we eat, we always want to eat what is sweet and tasty and avoid the opposite except a knowledgeable adult that eat what will make stay healthy.

Many adult live to eat and few adult eat to live. An adult that live to eat, eat only the sweet and avoid the sour but the adult that eat to live eat everything that lead to good health.

12

YOUR EMOTION AND YOUR HEALTH

God is a perfect God that make us according to his perfection and give us rules and regulation to live by if we want to live a well balanced life. If we neglect to live by the rules and regulation of God our life will be out of balance.

It is the emotion of jealousy that lead to the emotion of anger that make Cain to kill his brother Abel. If Cain was not jealous of his brother Abel in the first place, he will not have been angry to the point of killing his brother.

God is good and the word God was coined out of the word good and the devil is evil and the word devil was coin out of the word evil.

To be good is positive and to live positive and to be evil is negative and to live negative. When you are living a positive life, you will be of a good health and when you are living a negative life, you will be of a bad health and when your health is bad, your body will not be able to fight off coronavirus.

It is our emotion that govern us to be a positive person if the emotion is positive and if is also our emotion that govern us to be a negative person if the emotion is negative.

Anger, jealousy, hate, greed, lust, anxiety, procrastination, laziness, pride, arrogant, malicious, envy, attachment, are negative emotion and if we abhor them, we will become negative.

Love, patience, calmness, free giving, forgiveness, endurance, and any other positive trait that you can think of will make you a positive person if you can continuously dwell in them.

Negative emotion disrupt our digestive system and make our food not to digest well and if our food did not digest well, our body system will suffer the consequence.

Positive emotion make our digestive system to function well and make the small intestine to properly absorb the digested food which make our body organ to function properly and if our body organ function properly, then coronavirus will not be a threat to us.

Anger, jealousy, hatred and every other extreme negative emotion make us to lose vitamins and minerals through our skin and urine, although when they are excess in our body, we lose them through these channel.

If we exhibit extreme negative emotion, our body will rapidly lose vitamins and minerals in sweat and urine. If we continuously take them when we exhibit negative behavior, we will be similar to basket that water pass through it even if we continuously pour water into it.

13

MENTAL STRENGTH

We are spiritual being but science did not believe in spirit because they cannot investigate the human spirit nor any other spirit. There is no one that can scientifically prove the existence of a spirit but because we cannot prove the existence of a thing did not mean that it did not exist.

God is a spirit – John 4:24, and we are created in the likeness of God which make us also to be spirit.

We are body, soul, and spirit. Our body envelope our soul and our soul envelope our spirit. When God create us, God breathe his spirit into the nostril of man and man became a living soul, a soul that become a mind and animate the created body.

The Bible speak of a second death. The first death is the death of the body to release the soul (mind) and the second death is the death of the soul (mind) to release the human spirit either to go back to God to enjoy life for eternity or to go to hell for eternal destruction which is to cease to exist. Some religion assume hell to be a place of burning lake of fire but whatever you believe about hell, hell is not a place anyone should wish to see.

The strength of our life depend on the strength of our mind and the strength of our mind depend on the level of our knowledge and the level of our knowledge depend on the type of life that we are living.

A knowledgeable person live a positive life and put his or her life in order while an ignorant person live a negative life and his or her life is out of order.

If we have mental strength, we will not be afraid of coronavirus because we have knowledge and we know how to apply it in order to put coronavirus under control.

Coronavirus is not an enemy, it is an animal that is using human cell to stay alive just like every animal including we human that feed on another animal in order to stay alive.

We are intelligent being but coronavirus is not intelligent, so we should build the mental strength to live by the rules that will put coronavirus under control and eradicate it. To do this, we should avoid negative rumours and follow the guideline that will put coronavirus out of existence so that we can return to our normal life.

14

PUTTING CORONAVIRUS UNDER CONTROL

Coronavirus is a virus that don't like heat, it cannot survive a hot place for a long time. It like a cold place and can stay long in a cold place. We should therefore avoid a cold place and we should stop the use of the air conditioner and if we cannot tolerate too much heat, we should allow the atmosphere of a building or car to become hot for a period of time everyday. This means that we should learn to tolerate heat for the sake of our survival.

If we expose our environment to the hot air of the sun, the coronavirus will not stay long among us. If it can be possible let the bank and every governmental department ration the use of the air conditioner. Let us subject our environment to the heat of the sun and let us bear the heat of the sun so that we can eradicate the deadly coronavirus from our midst.

The second measure to take is to build our body defense mechanism by eating the type of food that will build our body defensive system.

The major symptom of coronavirus is difficulty in breathing when you exert yourself although low iron can also give this symptom but when this difficulty in breathing is accompany by a rise in body temperature, call 080097000010 and you will be ask some question to verify your symptom.

If you contact coronavirus, the earlier you start treatment, the better your chance of recovery but if you delay treatment because you think you will be stigmatize and the longer the virus stay with you, the difficult it will be to be treated and the more you are jeopardizing the life of people around you. What will you gain if you think you are going to die and you draw many people along with you?

15

THE CURE FOR CORONAVIRUS

Garlic is an antibacterial and it is a remedy for worm and onions have an edible acid. Since garlic is an antibacterial, it may also have effect on a weak virus like coronavirus.

Coronavirus is a weak virus that cannot stand a harsh and an acidic environment, therefore when eaten , it will get to the trachea to combact coronavirus from the inside and when an onions gas is inhale, it will combact coronavirus from the outside.

You must not eat a whole bulb of garlic because if you do, it will cause you allergic reaction. Eat a slice of it and do not eat more than your stomach can take.

To inhale the onions cut the onions into half and cut the base and press it to inhale the fume from one side of the nostril while blocking the other and do the same for the other side of the nostril. Why the base is preferable is that when you press the base, it will not scatter but when you press the upper side it will scatter unless you use your finger to guide it for it not to scatter.

Coronavirus is a weak virus that cannot stand the presence of garlic and onions, so it should be use on coronavirus patient and since they are edible, they will not have serious side effect on the human system.

I called it a cure because there is no other words that I can use to describe it to the understanding of everyone. It can only be called a cure when it have been tested and approved by the World Health Organization (WHO).

WHY IT IS DIFFICULT TO FIND A CURE

It is difficult to find a cure for coronavirus because a virus is not a cell unlike bacteria that is a cell.

A virus use the life of a cell for it own life therefore any drug that target to destroy it will also destroy the type of body cell that the virus is using for it own life. By changing the genome of a cell for it own life therefore will not withstand some chemistry that the body cannot withstand like garlic and onions which are food to our body but are acid to the coronavirus, then we can put an end to the deadly coronavirus.

Coronavirus is an animal that is trying to survive, it is not an enemy therefore let us bear this in mind so that we can be of a sane mind.

16

THE SOURCE OF FOOD THAT AID AGAINST CORONAVIRUS

VITAMIN A (RETINOL): It food source are liver, milk (some people stomach cannot tolerate milk, it bloat them), eggs, butter. Vitamin A is the most deficient vitamin in the human body because it cannot be adequately absorb in the small intestine without fatty food and anyone that lack vitamin B_{12} cannot tolerate fat which make the person to avoid fat which lead to deficiency of vitamin A.

Many people don't want to be fat which make them to avoid fatty food which cause them to be deficient in vitamin A. To be fat or lean have much to do with our gene. Those that have the gene for fat, their body will convert carbohydrate to fat to become fat when they avoid fat, so the only option for these people to remain lean is to starve themselves but starving oneself can generate a different type of health problem. If one's body convert carbohydrate to excess fat, there is a vitamin and mineral that the person lack that are suppose to put it under control.

Fat have earn a bad name because of it health related problem but we must eat a quantity of fat for our body to function well.

VITAMIN B_5 (PANTHENOL, PANTOTHENIC ACID, CALCIUM PANTOTHENATE): It food source are kidney, liver, whole grain, egg yolk, peanut, beef, turkey, chicken.

Vitamin B_5 food or supplement should not be eaten or taken alongside with vitamin C food or supplement because it acid destroy vitamin B_5.

VITAMIN B_{12} (CYANOCOBOLAMIN, COBOLAMIN): It food source are organ meat, liver, pork, fish, eggs. An intrinsic factor secreted by the stomach wall must be present for it absorption.

FOLIC ACID (FOLACIN, FOLATE): It food source are liver, whole grain, orange juice.

VITAMIN E (TOCOPHEROL): It food source are soya beans oil, peanut, whole grain, cabbage, egg.

CALCIUM: It food source are egg yolk, milk, fish eaten with bone, root, tubers, beans.

COPPER: It food source are legumes, nuts, mushroom, organ meat, seafood.

IODINE: It food source are iodized salt, seafood, garlic, eggs.

IRON: It food source are kidney, liver, lean meat, heart.
The absorption of iron depend on the level of iron in the blood. If the blood iron is high, the small intestine will not absorb iron. Iron are only absorb when the blood iron level is low and vitamin C aid the absorption of iron.
MAGNESIUM: If food source are grapefruit, chlorophyII from all plant, yellow corn, beans, brown rice, apple.
ZINC: It food source are milk, pumpkin seed, steamed crab, turkey, chicken, liver, egg.

These are the source of food that give the vitamins and minerals that the body need to fight against coronavirus but our food may not be able to give the highest amount needed to fight against the virus, so we need to supplement our food with vitamins and minerals supplement.
Vitamins and minerals supplement are digested supplement, so when we take them, they go directly to our body unlike food that have to be digested first before they go to our body and most time food are not completely digested before they pass out of the small intestine to large intestine where they become feaces. And some of these vitamins are destroyed by heat during cooking by overcooking.

17

SYMPTOM OF DEFICEINCY AND OVERDOSE

If we eat too much of a type of food, we will become a allergic to the food for the period of over eating the food and the allergic reaction will stop if we stop eating the food for a while for example eating too much of beans cause watery stooling for the period of over eating the beans. This is a way of our body to correct us that we need to eat other variety of food for our body to function properly.
As it is for the food that we eat, so is it for the vitamins and the minerals that we ingest.

As it is for eating too much type of a food, so it is for eating too little of a type of food.
When we eat too much type of a food, it affect our health and when we eat too little of a type of food, it also affect our health. A balance diet is what we need to eat for our body to function well.
VITAMIN A (RETINOL): Any dose higher than 25,000 IU daily for months will become toxic to the body and will become overdose and any dose that is lower than 5,000 IU daily is underdose and will create symptom of deficiency.
Symptom of deficiency are night blindness (inability to see in the night or in the dark especially when one move from a bright light to a dark place), dry eye, dry skin, dry mucous membrane, becoming easily infected with disease (especially respiratory, urogenital, and digestive tract infection), loss of taste and smell, defect in teeth and gum.
Symptom of overdose are nausea, vomiting, headache, hair loss, bone and joint pain, enlargement of liver and spleen, bone fragility.
VITAMIN B_5 (PANTHENOL, PANTOTHENIC ACID, CALCIUM PANTHOTENATE): Any dose lower then 10mg will create symptom of deficiency.
Symptom of deficiency are enlarge belly, duodenal ulcer, eczema, inflamation of the intestine and stomach, upper respiratory tract infection, constipation, allergies, graying hair, fatigue, pain in legs and arms.
There is no known symptom of overdose.
VITAMIN B_{12} (COBOLAMIN, CYNOCOBOLAMIN): Any dose lower than 6mcg will create symptom of deficiency.

Symptom of deficiency are weak pulse, numbness and tingling in extremites, drowsiness, irritability, chronic fatigue syndrome, paranoid psychosis, poor appetite, diarrhea, pernicious anemia.
There is no known symptom of overdose.
FOLIC ACID (FOLACIN, FOLATE): Any dose lower than 200 mcg for men and 180 mcg for women will create symptom of deficiency.
Symptom of deficiency are anemia, weakness, poor growth, numbness or tingling in hand and feet, depression, indigestion, diarrhea, mental illness, reduce resistance to infection, impaired wound healing, insomnia.
There is no known symptom of overdose.
VITAMIN C (ASCORBIC ACID): Depending on individual, dose higher than 6000 mg create symptom of overdose but the continuous dosage of 500mg daily for a long period of time will create the symptom of overdose and a dose less than 60 mg for a period of time create symptom of deficiency.
Symptom of deficiency are fleeting joint pain, poor teeth and bone growth, poor wound healing, low resistance to infection. Extreme deficit cause scurvy (bleeding gum, anemia, degeneration of muscle and cartilage, weight loss).
Symptom of overdose: enhanced mobilization of bone minerals and blood coagulation, exacbation of gout, kidney stone formation.
VITAMIN E (TOCOPHEROL): Any dose higher than 1,200 IU produce symptom of overdose, and a dose less than 30 IU produce symptom of deficiency.
Symptom of deficiency are: faulty fat absorption, degeneration of brain and spinal cord, decrease in sex hormones.
Symptom of overdose are: thrombophlebitis (inflammation of the wall of vein, hypertension, slow wound healing.
CALCIUM: A dose higher than 1,500 mg create symptom of overdose and a dose less than 300 mg produce symptom of deficiency.
Symptom of deficiency are: facial twitching, cramps, ricket, osteoporosis (porous and brittle bones), heart palpitation and slow pulse rate, osteomalacia (a bone softening disease), colon cancer.
Symptom of overdose are: depressed neural function, calcium salt deposit in soft tissues, kidney stone.
COPPER: A dose higher than 3mg produce symptom of overdose and a dose lower than 2mg produce symptom of deficiency. Copper should be taken with zinc at copper/zinc ration of 1:10.
Deficiency symptom are: anemia, brittle bone, loss of hair, loss of taste, general weakness, impaired respiration, chronic or recurrent diarrhea, low white blood cell count which lead to reduced resistance to infection, water retention, high cholesterol, development of ischemic heart disease, antacid use create copper deficiency .
Symptom of overdose are: abnormal storage which result in Wilson's disease.
IODINE: A dose higher than 300 mcg produce symptom of overdose and a dose lower than 80 mcg produce symptom of deficiency.
Symptom of deficiency are: goiter (enlarge thyroid gland), physical and mental sluggishness, restrict breathing and cause bulging of the eyes, poor circulation and low vitality, hypothyroidism (cold hand and feet and unable to tolerate cold weather), dry hair and skin, obesity, hearing loss.
Symptom of overdose: depresses synthesis of thyroid hormones.
IRON: The highest dose is hard to define because we all need iron according to our physical activities. An athlete need a high iron level for optimum athletic performance but any person

that do nothing need a low iron level. A dose lower than 10 mg will produce symptom of deficiency.
Symptom of deficiency: anemia (pallor, weakness, persistence fatigue, labored breathing on exertion, headache, palpitation), depressed immune system with decreased ability to produce white blood cells to fight off infection, gastrointestinal problem.
Symptom of overdose: damage to liver (cirrhosis), heart and pancreas, hardening of arteries.
MAGNESIUM: A dose higher than 750mg will produce symptom of overdose and a dose less than 280 mg will produce symptom of deficiency.
Symptom of deficiency: depression, confusion, vertigo (a condition where the room seem to spin round), disorientation, neuromuscular problem (muscular weakness and twitching, jumpiness), insomnia, sensitivity to noise, irritability, poor memory.
Symptom of overdose: diarrhea.
ZINC: A dose higher than 50 mg will produce symptom of overdose and a dose lower than 15 mg will produce symptom of deficiency. To be taken at zinc/copper ratio of 10:1.
Symptom of deficiency: loss of taste, smell and appetite, fingernails with white sport or bands, under developed penis and less full beard and underarm hair in boys, irregular menstrual circle in girls, infertility and impaired sexual function in adult, poor wound healing, skin lesions, stretch mark, loss of hair, increased susceptibility to infection, reduced salivation, reduced absorption of nutrient, retarted growth.
Symptom of overdose: difficult in walking, slurred speech, masklike facial expression, tremors.

Some people can be deficient in certain vitamin and mineral without showing deficiency symptom and some people may not be up to the level of deficiency but will exhibit deficiency symptom. These are base on the genetic makeup which make everyone to be individually different.

18

A LOOK INTO THE FUTURE

Knowledge is expensive but if you think that knowledge is too expensive and you neglect knowledge that is expensive to follow ignorance that cost nothing, what you will lose by the ignorance will be more expensive than the expensive knowledge that you neglect.

The Bible said that "my people die for lack of knowledge". For coronavirus to be put under control, my knowledge should not be neglected so that more people should not die from the hand of coronavirus and the untested cure of mine should not be neglected.

Beside this book that I did not plan to write that coronavirus lead me to writing it, it has also brought the plan of another book to my mind which is "LIVING A HEALTHY LIFE" but now I have a book which is "THE SECRET OF LIFE" which I suppose to have publish if not for the epidemic of coronavirus.
It is a book of over 150 pages and the chapters of the book are
1. The beginning of life. 2. The devil, a negative force. 3. Good and evil 4. The path to the light. 5. The law that govern life. 6. The secret of spiritual strength. 7. Fate. 8. The secret of time. 9. Prayer. 10. Reincarnation. 11. The secret of the conception of Christ. This book will be a marvel to the world and after reading it, you will agree with me that the book is a masterpiece that portray many hidden truth about life. Watch out for it, for it will be publish in hard copy after the coronavirus epidemic is over. Watch out for it in the net because it will follow up with the publication of this book in the Internet.

ABOUT THE AUTHOR

Raymond James was born in Ogbomosho, the then Oyo State in Nigeria to Mr. James Emezana and Mrs. Esther Emezana that both originated from Irri town in Delta State of Nigeria in 1974.My father was a soldier that jointhe Nigerian Army in 1963. As an Army children, wehave a good start in life but somewhere along the line after raising a good family my father resign from the Nigerian Army after serving for about 16 years to start a good trade. At first, my father was successful but after then, things start going against my father and we became a poor family.The poverty help to sharpen my brain because at an early age, I start to wonder why my parent are poor and many other parent are doing well in taking care of theirfamily and this form the foundation for the beginning of my knowledge.As a boy, during family discussions withfriends , We have always askedwho createdGod the creator of life and who createdthe creator?.When I become a young adult to my adult years,I start to search for the meaning of life and why some people seem to suffer and everything turn against them while some people enjoy and everything turn to their favor. With this, I discover a well of knowledge that lie deep down in my heart that I am gifted with knowledge and the result give birth to this book the secret of life.Although I could not forward my University Education after gaining admission to University of Benin in Nigeria due to the bad financial state of my parent which turn to my favorbecause the time I could have use
to study a particular field in my academic pursuit make me to study every book in different field of life which make me to be the jark of all trade but almost amaster in none.The money that I will make from this book Iwill use to study a particular field and be a master in the field which will remove me form the level of the master of none.

Raymond Elohoghene James Account Name: Raymond JamesAccount Number: 2266478603Bank Name: Zenith BankResidence Address: 12b behind No 12 Amame Street, Irri Delta State, Nigeria E-mail: goldenraymond123@gmail.comPassword: +2349072671121

MIX
Papier aus verantwortungsvollen Quellen
Paper from responsible sources
FSC® C105338

Printed by Books on Demand GmbH, Norderstedt / Germany